dieDASdocs

T0317846

Monumental Affairs_ Living with Contested Spaces

HATJE CANTZ

When we experienced the Saalecker Werkstätten together for the first time – its imposing ensemble looming over the Saale River near Naumburg – we quickly forged a plan to transform this historically troubled, "uncomfortable monument" into a sanctuary for contemporary cultural advancement. That moment in 2017 was the birth of dieDAS – Design Akademie Saaleck.

In 2018, Egidio Marzona acquired the historic site along with its dark and eventful history, inextricably entwined with the architect and racist ideologue Paul Schultze-Naumburg, and thus enabled the creation of the Marzona Stiftung Neue Saalecker Werkstätten (Marzona Foundation). In 1902, Schultze-Naumburg built his home in Saaleck and shortly afterwards founded the Saalecker Werkstätten, which soon became a platform for National Socialist propaganda and cultural politics. We felt strongly that the collective memory must never forget what evil was once expressed on these grounds.

As we write today, wars are raging, extreme right-wing parties are gaining strength, hate crimes are on the rise, and our environment is groaning under the gravity of the global climate crisis. In the context of these immense challenges, we are called to question the causes while at the same time envisioning innovative solutions. This effort requires both a critical examination of our past and the promotion of forward-looking ideas. It is at this interface that dieDAS is active.

The academy was founded to offer designers and other creatives opportunities for development, research, and networking, rooted in the deep conviction that spaces of open exchange are essential to the design of paradigm-shifting and socially relevant processes capable of enriching our present and future coexistence. Accordingly, the Marzona Foundation has established dieDAS as a new space for free thought, experimentation, and interdisciplinary discourse that brings together a diverse international community of scholars, designers, architects, craftspeople, artists, scientists, partner institutions, and more to explore urgent topics, from material ecology, sustainability, and organic design to climate, justice, and democracy.

dieDAS has been hosting events since 2019. At the annual Open House, we invite interested parties from Saaleck and the surrounding area to explore the site and personally experience its evolution. Together with the dieDAS team and our rotating artistic directors – to date acclaimed designers Maurizio Montalti (2020–22) and Germane Barnes (2023–24) – we have developed two formats for the international creative community: the dieDAS Fellowship Program and the dieDAS walk + talk Symposium. We are proud of the impressive roster of leading-edge thinkers and practitioners that these events have already engaged and grateful for the participants' ongoing collaboration.

With this publication, we have the opportunity not only to reflect on what dieDAS has accomplished in its first few years but also to delve deeper into our latest area of focus, Monumental Affairs: Living with Contested Places, the theme of our 2023 fellowship program and walk + talk Symposium led by Barnes.

In his role as dieDAS Artistic Director, Barnes has chosen to interrogate monuments from a sociopolitical perspective and to understand architecture as a vehicle for an alternative historiography. Through our programs, the Monumental Affairs theme confronts the legacy of contaminated pasts that live on in our built environment and examines the narratives, purposes, and canonization of buildings and monuments in a range of contexts. Vital questions include: Who determines what architecture enters the canon, and how? What overt and subtle forms of oppression are at work? And in what ways can the concept of public space be used to dismantle contested monuments?

dieDAS promotes change with the aim of transforming our own historically contaminated site into a cultural beacon whose light may be visible far beyond the borders of Saaleck and Naumburg. We are at the beginning of a multiyear renovation project following a design by Danish architect Dorte Mandrup. In the coming years, the old buildings will gradually be put to new use so that more and more events, workshops, and thematically relevant explorations can be offered to local and international communities. This vision would not be possible without the decisive support of the State of Saxony-Anhalt and the Federal Republic of Germany accompanied by a growing number of committed partners from Germany and abroad.

In the heart of Germany, dieDAS – Design Akademie Saaleck intends to set a resolute and tangible example in Europe and the world for unrestricted creative freedom and for the power of change in a democratic society.

Egidio Marzona, Andreas Silbersack, Arne Cornelius Wasmuth
Board of Directors, Marzona Foundation

FOREWORD

INTRODUCTION

Monumental Affairs: Living with Contested Spaces asks a fundamental question: What is a monument? Traditionally, the term connotes structures designed with the explicit intention to express and instill respect for people, places, and events that have impacted the societies that surround them. By convention, monuments are conceived as permanent, unchanging, and highly visible invocations to current and future generations to never forget the values imparted by the memorialized subjects.

The agency to bestow official monumental status – and therefore to decide which communal virtues are most worthy of celebration and preservation – has historically belonged to those who wield the most economic, social, and political power. Consequently, the most visible and imposing monuments, along with the values they embody, often serve to reinforce existing hierarchies, entrenching unjust systems bent on suppressing marginalized and dissenting voices. Today, amid heightened critiques of the enduring effects of deeply rooted inequities, exploitation, and erasure, the traditional definition of what constitutes a monument, and who decides, has begun to crumble.

Against this critical backdrop, this volume – the first book published by dieDAS – Design Akademie Saaleck – adopts an expansive, progressive interpretation of monuments in order to probe another, more complex question: If monuments are understood as the embodiments of a society's collective memory, shared ideals, and unifying identity, how then can they be conceptualized, constructed, and preserved to represent a greater diversity of perspectives, disrupt oppressive power structures, and promote positive change in a world rife with compounding social and environmental crises?

The title and topic of *Monumental Affairs_Living with Contested Spaces* are inspired by the theme that dieDAS Artistic Director Germane Barnes chose for the institution's 2023 fellowship program and walk + talk Symposium. Through the discursive framework outlined in his curatorial statement and developed in his 2023 curriculum at dieDAS, the Miami-based architect and educator invited the programs' participants to explore facets of monuments and monument-making beyond conventional definitions, recognizing the existence of many kinds of monuments – formal and informal, intentional and unintentional, beneficial and harmful – and their relationship to issues surrounding race, immigration, displacement, and nationalism, among others.

An essential principle lies at the heart of Barnes's theme: the structures we erect are intrinsically entwined with the values we most honor. Through this lens, the mutable and subjective nature of monumentality comes into focus. As a society evolves over time, the monuments of its past are inevitably reassessed, even contested; demands to erect new and destroy old monuments emerge and compete; and existing structures acquire monument-like meanings that they were not originally designed to express. When we examine more closely the feedback loop between what we collectively value and what we collectively build, our understanding of monumentality widens even further. We begin to see that monuments exist around us everywhere, wherever communities feel the impact of cultural, economic, and political ideologies manifested in their physical surroundings. Our cities, landscapes, and homes are all monuments, of a kind, to the systems in which they were shaped.

Section I of this book, entitled "Monumental Affairs," expounds on Barnes's multidimensional theme, illuminating our understanding of monuments through five distinct yet complementary, thought-provoking, and timely essays. Of the five contributors included in this section, it should be noted, the first four also spoke at dieDAS's 2023 walk + talk Symposium, including Barnes himself.

Barnes's essay, "The Power of Architecture," unpacks the personal experiences that magnified for him the myriad ways that architecture, in theory and practice, has the capacity to either perpetuate or push back against the power structures that engender systems of segregation and oppression—a focus that in turn informed his vision for dieDAS's 2023 programming. In "Memory Is Momentum," New Orleans–based architect and design justice advocate Bryan C. Lee, Jr., also shares a poignant, personal account, revealing how his great-grandfather's appalling experience as a Black man buying a home in a white neighborhood is emblematic of the white supremacist ideology etched into US-America's built fabric. Lee champions design as a tool of protest, a weapon in the arsenal against entrenched systems that withhold wealth, health, and opportunity from Black and Brown communities.

Paris-based architect and urban planner Meriem Chabani's essay, "Sanctuaries of Care in Uncertain Times," argues that our current global crises, from climate change to widespread social unrest, are the inevitable outcome of capitalist hegemony, fueled by a venal ethos that regards everything on earth as fodder for exploitation in pursuit of limitless economic growth. The path towards a more just and resilient world, according to Chabani, begins by cultivating a culture of care for the planet and all its inhabitants, which entails designating some resources as sacred, inviolate, off-limits for temporal gain. Magdeburg-based Professor of Sociology Matthias Quent likewise lays bare the deleterious impacts of inhumane and oppressive worldviews, in particular reactionary, right-wing sociopolitical movements cloaked in the language of nature conservation. His essay, "Spaces and Ideologies of Inequality in the Climate Crisis," warns against the insidious, pseudoscientific lies that underpin eat-or-be-eaten social Darwinism and xenophobic eco-fascism and perpetuate untold acts of violence against both people and the environment.

Cambridge-based architect and academic Sarah M. Whiting, Dean of Harvard Graduate School of Design (GSD) and member of the dieDAS

Advisory Board, concludes the first section of this publication with "Monumental Consistencies and Complexities." Here, Whiting reviews important debates over monument-making from the last century of architectural history alongside promising currents in twenty-first-century discourse and practice – including work being done at Harvard GSD and dieDAS. Like the other contributors to this publication, she underscores the need for architects and designers to consider not only the functions that our built environments fulfill, but also the values that they express.

Importantly, Barnes's Monumental Affairs theme dovetails with die-DAS's overarching mission – beyond the 2023 programming – and shines a light on the twofold, interconnected mandates conceived at the institution's foundation five years ago by the Marzona Foundation. On the one hand, dieDAS is an academy dedicated to bringing together interdisciplinary, intersectional practitioners and thinkers working at the leading edge of design, architecture, and craft to explore forward-facing, socially conscious approaches to urgent global issues in an atmosphere of open exchange. At the same time, dieDAS exists to confront the dark history of the site that it calls home, the Saalecker Werkstätten, which was designed and built by racist idealogue Paul Schultze-Naumburg just after the turn of the twentieth century and survives today as an "uncomfortable monument." This publication, therefore, continues with a series of essays and interviews that reflect on dieDAS's ambitious vision for building a reconciliatory bridge between the horrific failures of the past and humanity's highest aspirations for the future by harnessing the power of education, dialogue, and creative collaboration.

Section II, "Saalecker Werkstätten," delves into the sensitive steps that dieDAS is undertaking to disarm the uncomfortable monument status of its campus. In her essay, "The Making of an Uncomfortable Monument," Daniela Spiegel, Professor of Heritage Conservation and Architectural History at the Bauhaus-Universität Weimar, traces the hateful history of the Saalecker Werkstätten and explains why the harm that was inflicted by its architect should neither be erased from collective memory nor uplifted through traditional monumental framing. As an uncomfortable monument, the site must be transformed to benefit society in direct contradiction to the racist, antisemitic values once espoused there. In "The Transformation of an Uncomfortable Monument," Stephan Kujas, Monument Conservator for the City of Weißenfels, outlines how dieDAS is meeting this objective, both through the creation of an archival research center that preserves knowledge of the site's past as well as through its repurposing in the service of nurturing positive outcomes for the wider world. Penned by Copenhagen-based architect Dorte Mandrup, "Exposing, Leaving, Adding" previews the Saalecker Werkstätten's next, transformative chapter. Mandrup's renovation design, which will be completed in a few years, will allow dieDAS to welcome larger audiences in Saaleck and amplify its values-driven mission.

Section III, entitled "dieDAS – Design Akademie Saaleck," surveys the progress that dieDAS has made in its crucial, first five years, articulated through a collection of interviews with some of the team members and participants who have played key roles in bringing the young academy's mission to life. As an ensemble, these first-hand accounts constitute a cross-sectional oral history of the conceptualization and implementation of dieDAS's central initiatives, including the annual fellowship program and walk + talk Symposium, among others. These voices bear witness to the earnest, collaborative spirit that suffuses dieDAS's programming, painting a heartfelt picture of the impacts already felt within the community alongside the advancements we can expect from the academy in the near and long terms.

Every year, a fresh cohort of international fellows, mentors, speakers, and visitors assemble at dieDAS to question and reinvigorate the site anew, leveraging design's boundless creative toolbox to break down and reimagine topics of far-reaching resonance. Rather than museumize the Saalecker Werkstätten or obscure their dark legacy, dieDAS is committed to transforming a monument of pain into an emblem of hope; an evolving learning space that facilitates clear-eyed assessments of living histories; and a dynamic design laboratory where prescient and passionate talents representing diverse perspectives, experiences, and expertise cooperate to envision a more just, equitable, and sustainable future. Within this specific microcosm, at the nexus of these creative and cultural exchanges, dieDAS and its expanding community of collaborators are working to build a world that honors humanity's loftiest values.

Anna Carnick and Wava Carpenter
Curators, Editors, and Cofounders of Anava Projects

Table of Contents

I. Monumental Affairs

Monumental Affairs: Living with Contested Spaces
The 2023 dieDAS Fellowship Program Thematic Statement

As historically excluded voices increasingly expose the failures and discriminatory practices of the architecture and urbanism fields, a holistic, constructive examination of these disciplines becomes all the more pressing. Global terror and dissent typically identified as political and militaristic have slowly revealed their spatial influences. Design justice continues to peak through creases often closed shut by popular architectural theory and discourse. This shift towards a more egalitarian and non-Western intellectual approach is the impetus for the 2023 iteration of the dieDAS Fellowship, Monumental Affairs. Within this framework, designers, theorists, architects, critics, and beyond are challenged to posit the necessity of monuments.

Monumental Affairs asks: How does the process of canonization come to fruition? Who determines which architecture becomes part of the canon? What overt or subtle forms of oppression are inherent in this process? How does one utilize the public sphere to dismantle these canonized monuments?

Situated in Saaleck, Germany, at the former home of German architect and racist idealogue Paul Schultze-Naumburg (and a one-time hub for the country's totalitarian National Socialists), dieDAS presents fellows a fraught yet fertile environment in which to deploy acts of tactical urbanism as a means of architectural and spatial resistance. During their stay, the interdisciplinary cohort will attempt to use architecture as a vehicle for alternative histories. The speculation of design ideas will support workshops surrounding race, ethnicity, immigration, displacement, and nationalism. Monumental Affairs acknowledges the nationalist agenda of this historic site, its contested legacy, and its explicit exclusion of non-white constructors.

By addressing these issues directly – and mindful of the urgency and opportunity posed by our current global climate – dieDAS aims to cultivate an environment of rigor, reflection, and imagination.

Germane Barnes
dieDAS Artistic Director 2023–24

1

1. dieDAS Fellowship Program 2023, Monumental Affairs participants: (back to front) Director of Program & Development Tatjana Sprick, Founding Director Arne Cornelius Wasmuth, Artistic Director Germane Barnes, Fellow Antoinette Yetunde Oni, Head Mentor Zeno Franchini, Fellow Adam Maserow, Fellow Yassine Ben Abdallah, and Fellow Silvia Susanna

2. dieDAS Fellowship Program 2023 excursion to Saaleck Castle: (left to right) Mentor Mo Asumang, Fellow Silvia Susanna, Fellow Antoinette Yetunde Oni, Fellow Yassine Ben Abdallah, Head Mentor Zeno Franchini, Artistic Director Germane Barnes, Fellow Adam Maserow
3. dieDAS Artistic Director Germane Barnes with 2023 Fellows Silvia Susanna, Adam Maserow, Yassine Ben Abdallah

5. Workshop led by Colin Hacklander and Farahnaz Hatam of Studio Labour during the dieDAS Fellowship Program 2023
6. Mentor Kenny Cupers in conversation with Fellow Adam Maserow during the dieDAS Fellowship Program 2023

7. Workshop led by Ido Nahari, editor of *Arts of the Working Class*, during the dieDAS Fellowship Program 2023
8. Head Mentor Zeno Franchini in conversation with Mentor Kenny Cupers and Fellow Antoinette Yetunde Oni during the dieDAS Fellowship Program 2023

9. Monumental Affairs project by 2023 Fellow Adam Maserow
10. Monumental Affairs project by 2023 Fellow Antoinette Yetunde Oni

1. 2023 Fellow Silvia Susanna in conversation with Curator and Editor Anna Carnick
2. Monumental Affairs project by 2023 Fellow Yassine Ben Abdallah

13

13. Monumental Affairs dieDAS walk + talk Symposium 2023

14

15

14. Bryan C. Lee, Jr., speaking at the dieDAS walk + talk Symposium 2023
15. Matthias Quent speaking at the dieDAS walk + talk Symposium 2023

Germane Barnes

Architect, Founder of Studio Barnes,
Associate Professor and Director of The Community Housing
and Identity Lab at the University of Miami School of Architecture,
and dieDAS Artistic Director (2023–24)

The Power
of Architecture

My life was forever changed on September 9, 2004. That day, I received a phone call from my father, informing me that my older sister had lost her battle with cancer. I was in my first year of college, studying architecture at the University of Illinois at Urbana-Champaign. It was early in the morning. I recall this detail because after ending the call in a state of shock, I put on my clothes and attended Design Studio 1, which began at 9 a.m.

I've always wanted to be an architect. After losing my sister, though, my relationship with architecture fractured. I'd always been a strong, driven student, but now I struggled to focus on my studies and couldn't regain the excitement and tenacity that filled me prior to arriving on campus. As I neared graduation, I realized I would not be able to gain admittance into graduate school with scores and a portfolio that were inarguably subpar. So I decided to postpone graduate pursuits and explore immediate employment. This led to my first internship in Cape Town, at an architecture firm that specialized in high-end residential projects and pro bono work in impoverished areas. And that was my turning point.

It was there, in the township of Khayelitsha, providing architecture and design aid to forcibly displaced, underserved communities, that I became aware of socially engaged design. That is where I learned the power of architecture: its ability to subjugate and oppress – and, conversely, to uplift. Witnessing firsthand the stark disparities in access to resources and opportunities ignited a passion within me to use design to address systemic injustices and empower marginalized communities.

16.
Germane Barnes

I'd always been a careful observer of the built environment. As a child, I spent hours each day traversing my hometown of Chicago on a bus to and from school, from the far west side where I lived to the north side and later downtown, watching the cityscape shift from workforce housing to elegant single-family homes and massive towers that oftentimes people who look like me could not dream of affording. But my education in South Africa provided me with a clear sense of agency. This experience became the spark that has since animated my entire architecture and research approach, fueled by an imperative to harness architecture as a tool for social change. My life experiences have instilled in me a commitment to equity, sustainability, and human dignity, manifested in a practice that centers collaboration and community to design spaces that empower, heal, and foster social cohesion. This drives me to advocate for inclusive design practices and an expansion of the architectural canon that prioritizes and foregrounds the needs and voices of those habitually ignored by a Western-focused pedagogy.

17.
For the 18th Venice Biennale of Architecture, Studio Barnes created *Griot*, speculating on legacies missing from the foundational architectural canon

The field of architecture has long been dominated by white perspectives, resulting in a profound lack of representation for Black architects. This underrepresentation not only reflects broader systemic inequalities but also perpetuates a cycle of marginalization within the built environment. Architecture, as a form of cultural expression and a tool of power, plays a significant role in shaping the social, economic, and spatial dynamics of communities. Highways plow through neighborhoods, eminent domain "justifies" destruction, and gentrification drives displacement. Concrete behemoths, while providing public infrastructure, can also be viewed as memorials given their monumentality. They are the embodiment and symbols of dominance and force. In these circumstances, architecture actively contributes to the silencing and erasure of minority voices by reinforcing existing power structures and perpetuating spatial segregation.

18.
Germane Barnes speaking at dieDAS's 2023 walk + talk Symposium on the theme Monumental Affairs

It is for this reason that the Monumental Affairs program was envisioned. It is impossible to visit the compound created by a racist ideologue in Saaleck, Germany, and not view the site through the lens of oppression. Paul Schultze-Naumburg's legacy is one of hate, materialized as a Frankenstein structure around a sculpted garden. Here, formal and informal historical markers collide, as do conversations about labor, migration, xenophobia, and beyond. It is, frankly, a monument.

Monuments stand as tangible symbols of history, culture, and power, but they can also exist as contested sites where narratives of colonialism and racism intersect – and can be addressed and challenged. Throughout history, monuments have been erected to commemorate individuals, events, or ideologies, often reflecting the values of the dominant groups in society. However, many of these monuments celebrate figures who were implicated in colonial exploitation, slavery, and other forms of oppression. This site, dieDAS, is no different. Hitler himself was once welcomed here.

The continued existence of such monuments in the built environment can perpetuate a legacy of inequality and injustice, reinforcing narratives that marginalize or erase the experiences of oppressed communities. They can also serve as reminders of historical injustices and the ongoing struggles for equality and justice – and, in instances, provide a framework for constructive discourse. Within the Monumental Affairs Fellowship Program, we invited voices from all over the globe to engage the site and share a range of perspectives that allowed for robust conversations about power dynamics and design as a responsive tool. Musicians, artists, theorists, and other creatives utilized this location as a point of departure to interrogate the social and political influence of monuments worldwide.

> "Ultimately, the significance of monuments lies not only in their physical presence but also in the conversations and actions they inspire."

In Saaleck, as around the globe, monuments have become a focal point of public debate and activism, as communities grapple with questions of representation, memory, and identity. Ultimately, the significance of monuments lies not only in their physical presence but also in the conversations and actions they inspire. By engaging with monuments as contested sites, societies have the opportunity to confront difficult truths, challenge dominant narratives, and strive towards a more just and equitable future. That is necessary. That is what lies at the heart of the dieDAS vision.

Bryan C. Lee, Jr.

NOMA, AIA, Founder/Design Principal of Colloqate, and Design Justice Advocate

Memory is Momentum

Just after noon on August 16, 1960, a letter was mailed to a new home-owner in Hamilton Township, New Jersey, USA. This area was considered, at the time, an all-white neighborhood with a designated C rating from the Federal Housing Authority, meaning it was a middling neighborhood with little to no infiltration of Black or Brown people. Penned by anonymous neighbors, the threatening letter was received by Roderick Woodard, a forty-six-year-old postal worker, a Black man with four children, trying to live a better life. Roderick had purchased the house less than a month prior to receiving the letter, and in those few weeks of ownership, the property was covered with racist graffiti, saw multiple cross burnings, and was finally the target of an arson fire. Roderick was my great-grandfather.

19.
AI + Photoshop collage of Roderick Woodard, Lee's great-grandfather, alongside the letter he received and related newspaper clippings

In that era (and even now), Black people have often faced similar challenges to finding safe, affordable housing. The realty company expressed no concerns from the neighbors to Roderick, but unfortunately, those very same neighbors sought retribution for the sale almost immediately. Within thirty days of buying a new home, my great-grandfather was confronted with the compounding injustice ingrained into our nation's social, political, economic, and spatial systems.

A historically racist social system viewed him as less than worthy of dignity and humanity. A political system ensured that these beliefs made their way into racialized housing covenants and eventually into the federal policy of redlining. An economic system, built off the labor of our ancestors, incentivized the differential valuation of land and property based on race and class. And a segregated spatial system used the boundaries of land and property to enforce and subsequently validate all other systems.

This is just one of many stories like it, but one worthy of remembering as it gives insight into the structure of the world we've created. I believe that for nearly every injustice we see in this world, there is architecture, a plan, and a design built to sustain it.

My work advocates for dismantling the privilege and power structures that use architecture and design as tools of oppression. It makes clear architecture's role in creating spaces of liberation through the narratives of people, place, and power, all juxtaposed at a greater frequency than chance.

The maintenance of oppressive ideologies depends on a society's ability to construct a collective narrative, memorialize those beliefs into the infrastructures that shape our world, and consequently erase all imprints of alternative cultures, histories, and values.

If we tell ourselves the story that some people are more worthy of housing than others, then we build housing markets that keep people on the edge of poverty while promoting housing and homeless crises. If we tell ourselves the story that our communities should be segregated from one another, then we build neighborhoods, housing, roads, stores, and schools that affirm that separation.

If we tell ourselves that some people are more dangerous than others, then we create systems of policing that feed the prison industrial complex, which is sustained by the development of spaces that drain social and economic potential from marginalized people. If we convince ourselves of the story that our environment is not impacted by our presence, then we continue to extract from the land, overconsume our forests, and build buildings that demand an outsized and unsustainable share of our world's energy production.

When we tell ourselves these stories, our collective values are validated through the spaces and places that we design. We must recognize that within racist systems we build spaces as monuments in memory to the hubris of white supremacy.

The force of these issues may seem insurmountable, but the memories we keep and the collection of memories we construct in response to prevailing conditions will define the worlds we are to build in the future. If the root of all oppression is the loss of memory, then the root of all liberation must be the relentless preservation and making of memory – in language, in stories, in place, and in culture.

The practice of design justice carries with it the belief that the language we use to tell the stories of place is essential. Architecture is a language. Like all languages, it allows us to hold complex narratives capable of honoring the importance of all of our stories.

Stories engrain themselves in place – into our neighborhoods, our blocks, and buildings – and turn memory to monument, because place impacts our day-to-day lived experiences and the cultural narratives we allow to persist.

For communities of color in US-America, there is power in the places and spaces where our culture is recognized, where our stories are told, and where our language is valued. Like the griots of Mali in West Africa, the built environment is a documentarian, a witness to inequality and injustice, joy and resilience, pain and pleasure. It is a storyteller, a container of moments and memory preserved to shine light on our path through a relentless world. It is said that when a griot dies, a library burns to the ground.

20.
Remember When.
Remember Then.
Collage by Bryan C. Lee, Jr.
/ Colloqate Design

The gravity of the metaphor has always grounded me in the simple notion that memory is momentum; it propels us collectively forward, allowing words to travel through time and tongue, relying on the fidelity of our connections in community to breathe meaning into meaningless symbols and life back into lifeless spaces. Without it, we are destined to stall out.

Architects, planners, and urbanists are responsible for interpreting and translating the continuous dialogue between the cultural interactions of place and the architectural language of place, and in so doing, allowing the mythologies in our memory to live on in perpetuity.

Herein lies the underlying prompt of design justice. These issues are complex in and of themselves, but the combinatorial impact on marginalized communities is often too much to bear. Our work seeks to envision spaces of social, cultural, and economic justice as an act of reparation and healing.

If I can leave you with one thing: The values that we embody in our social constructs become the values embedded in our physical constructs. The art and architecture of our built environment are inextricably linked to our social existence, yet the depths of this relationship sit on the periphery of our conversations about racism and oppression.

Ultimately, I view design as a tool of protest; to protest is to have an unyielding faith in the power and potential to build a just society. It is fundamentally about a collective hope for a shared future, propelled by a shared history. At its very best, design is the physical manifestation of our collective memory made manifest in pursuit of a more just and liberated world.

This essay is excerpted from Lee's forthcoming book, *Power + Place*.

Meriem Chabani

Partner at TXKL and President of New South

Sanctuaries of Care in Uncertain Times

The Global North holds little space for the sacred. In the wake of its centuries-long hegemony, we all are now faced daily with a world shaped by capital, the driving force behind the making of our cities, our homes, and our everyday lives. The valuation of wealth and unchecked growth above all else has delivered us into an era marked by rampant inequity, widespread social upheaval, and an existential climate emergency. How do we construct an equivalent yet more humane system of value that can stand face-to-face with such a powerful, destructive force? How can honoring the sacred – the *inviolable* – help us build a better world?

Artist, writer, activist, and architectural researcher Imani Jacqueline Brown investigates the legacy of plantations and the traces left by enslaved populations along Louisiana's Mississippi River in the US. This territory over time has transitioned from "Plantation Country" to "Petrochemical Corridor," also known as "Cancer Alley," as brutalizing sugarcane farms have been replaced with polluting petrochemical facilities, resulting in some of the country's most toxic air and highest cancer rates. Throughout, the Black communities who live there have suffered the fallout.

21.
Kursi by New South imagines furniture as an invitation to gather in conversation or quiet contemplation; when stacked, the simple stools form columns to mark out a sacred space

In the center of Brown's research site are burial grounds, which were uncovered during surveys for a proposed refinery expansion; they are presumably among the hundreds, if not thousands, of other, hidden ancestral sites in peril of desecration. Working together with activist group RISE St. James and research studio Forensic Architecture, Brown's efforts have revealed stark examples of environmental racism – byproducts of colonialism and slavery – and advocate for the need to locate additional cemeteries and enact a moratorium on the further expansion of the petrochemical industry.[1] This recovered sacred space, withstanding the test of time, lays bare the distance between two contradictory value systems, one driven by capital and the other by care.

Meanwhile, in his 2021 book *The States of the Earth* (*Des empires sous la terre*), philosopher Mohamed Amer Meziane offers a racial and

1. Imani Jacqueline Brown, Samaneh Moafi, and Forensic Architecture in partnership with RISE St. James, *Environmental Racism in Death Alley, Louisiana: Phase I Investigative Report*, July 4, 2021, https://content.forensic-architecture.org/wp-content/uploads/2021/07/Environmental-Racism-in-Death-Alley-Louisiana_Phase-1-Report_Final_2021.07.04.pdf (accessed April 24, 2024).

ecological reading of the nineteenth-century secularization of Europe. He establishes a parallel between the disassociation from religious or spiritual concerns and the rise of colonial capitalist extractivism, neoliberalism, and deregulation. Penning the concept of the "Secularocene," he argues that as belief in the heavenly dominion over earth began to be replaced by materialistic, imperialistic ideologies, the ground beneath our feet (along with its rich mineral resources) lost all links with the transcendent divine, which left the earth open to boundless commodification and extraction. Or, in the words of Meziane, "It is the critique of Heaven that has shaken the Earth."[2]

In my own work, I am interested in investigating ways in which traditional, sacred practices can be manifested and preserved in the built environment to embrace new and forgotten sustainable approaches to architecture and city-making. In the face of deep, interrelated social and environmental crises, there is a pressing need to cultivate a renewed vision of an aspirational modernity. In a sense, we need a Sacred Green New Deal.

To define the sacred, we need to look beyond religion and focus instead on care: What have people protected and maintained across time and contexts? What is (and should be) left untouched and undefiled? We must start by recognizing the existence of sacred practices worldwide. From Standing Rock to the Brazilian Amazon, Indigenous peoples have long led the fight against extractive and destructive land exploitation. Melissa K. Nelson, an ecologist and native scholar-activist, makes a case for the restoration of Indigenous stewardship of land and water. "We Indigenous peoples have cultural and spiritual obligations to embody Indigenous ideals of interrelations and to restore the balance between people and place."[3] In that regard, the Global South holds significant resources to help us understand how sacredness and the built environment can intertwine and thrive.

One example can be found in the Algerian desert, in the oasis town of Ghardaia. A few decades ago, the townspeople decided to expand their settlement beyond the historical city walls, cutting down the surrounding palm grove to make room for new housing. In 2008, heavy rainfall resulted in a catastrophic flood that destroyed hundreds of homes and killed dozens of people. The neighboring town of Beni Isguen, however, which had preserved the trees growing on its border, was much less affected by the torrential downpour. Recognizing the contrast, the people of Ghardaia and many in the wider region reestablished their fundamental relationship with the palm tree and the important role it plays in guarding their communities.[4] The palm tree was

2. Mohamed Amer Meziane, *The States of the Earth: An Ecological and Racial History of Secularization*, trans. Jonathan Adjemian (London: Verso, 2024); first published as *Des empires sous la terre, Histoire écologique et raciale de la sécularisation* (Paris: La Découverte, 2021).

3. Melissa K. Nelson, "Time to Indigenize Conservation: Native American Activists Are Leading a Push to Embed Traditional Ecological Knowledge in Land Management Decisions," *Sierra* (January/ February 2021), December 22, 2020, https://www.sierraclub.org/sierra/2021-1-january-february/feature/time-indigenize-lands-and-water-conservation (accessed April 26, 2024).

4. UNESCO World Heritage Convention; Climate Change Case Studies, "Promoting Traditional Environmental Knowledge in the M'Zab Valley (Algeria)," https://whc.unesco.org/en/canopy/mzab/ (accessed April 24, 2024).

deemed, if not holy, then undoubtedly an object of sacred significance. Here, sanctuarization was deployed with relative success for the care of natural reserves. And yet the story of Ghardaia teaches another lesson: Constructing a sanctuary doesn't inherently involve detachment from the urban landscape; rather, it underscores the exigency of interconnectedness. Building sanctuaries is a way to define, collectively, priorities that are absolute.

Sanctuarization is gaining traction worldwide, through movements like the 30x30 initiative, an international coalition dedicated to achieving governmental protection of 30% of the earth's land and sea by 2030.[5] From this perspective, sacredness is framed not only as environmentally and socially mindful, but also as an economic principle: by design, the sacred is what exceeds the reach of temporal, economic exchanges. Translated into the language of contemporary architecture, the sacred is outside of the grasp of unchecked real-estate development and unlimited, unsustainable material exploitation.

22.
Walled city of Ghardaia, Algeria

Consider the Great Mosque of Djenné in Mali, a Saharan example of collective care. Each year, every member of the Djenné community takes part in the annual renovation of the historic, adobe structure, preparing and applying the earth daub to combat heavy erosion.[6] Through generations of collective care, the holiness of the mosque is reaffirmed as a cornerstone of the city's identity that brings its citizens together around a central project. Through the shared guardianship of the building by its community, new possibilities for sustainable practices in the built environment emerge.

Around the globe, instances of the sacred offer guidance for reclaiming our connection to one another and the earth. Reinstating these cosmogonies may help us navigate the Secularocene, allowing us to break free from barren grounds by rebuilding sanctuaries, restoring sacred covenants between people and place, and fostering truly sustainable cities.

5. Eric Dinerstein et al., "A Global Deal For Nature: Guiding Principles, Milestones, and Targets," *Science Advances*, April 19, 2019, https://www.science.org/doi/10.1126/sciadv.aaw2869 (accessed April 24, 2024).
6. The Children's Museum of Indianapolis, "The Great Mosque of Djenné," *Sacred Places*, https://sacredplacesexhibit. org/mali/ (accessed April 24, 2024); and Jehan Alfarra, "Discover the Great Mosque of Djenne, Mali," *MEMO Middle East Monitor*, July 4, 2021, https://www.middleeastmonitor.com/20210704-discover-the-great-mosque-of-djenne-mali/ (accessed April 24, 2024).

Prof. Dr.

Matthias Quent

Professor of Sociology, Magdeburg-Stendal University of Applied Sciences

Spaces and Ideologies of Inequality in the Climate Crisis

It is wonderful that the Design Akademie in Saaleck – a place where the past and present palpably coexist – is creating something new. One hundred years ago, this site – a place set between the forest, mountains, and the Saale River, somewhat removed from the centers of modernity yet conveniently situated at the crossroads of important arteries – was occupied by Paul Schultze-Naumburg, who proved to be a rabid racist and antisemite. On the extreme right today, he is invoked positively as a genuinely right-wing ecologist. The responsibility and opportunity to reexamine the relationship between fascism, the environment, spatial design, and the process of modernization is thus inherent in this location.

Around the turn of the twentieth century, Schultze-Naumburg helped organize the Bund Heimatschutz (Association of Homeland Security), a body that not only advocated for regional protection of the environment, but also regarded itself as a resolute opponent of industrial progress. Members of the Bund Heimatschutz saw the capitalist industrial state as a threat to indigenous nature, as well as to the German national identity and the soul of the German people. In his day, Schultze-Naumburg campaigned against the industrial use of the Rhine River for a large hydroelectric power plant, among other things. He would surely argue against wind power stations today. And as a person who railed against "cultural bolshevism" and "modernism," he would certainly disparage the diversity of the Design Akademie Saaleck and its progressive programming as well.

The fact that, a century after the rise of National Socialism in Germany, right-wing extremists in Europe and North America continue to revile people as "cultural Marxists" and to attack and even murder them calls into question the West's much-extolled reappraisal of the past. What is shocking about the old texts by Schultze-Naumburg is not only his racism, but also how topical the discursive pattern of culturally based racism is today, echoing not only on the extreme right but also at the center of Western societies.

As a result of his extreme racism and active support for the National Socialist regime, Schultze-Naumburg was among those intellectuals who bore responsibility for the mass murder of Jews, non-white individuals, homosexuals, Sinti and Roma, the ill, people with disabilities, leftists, artists, intellectuals, and others. Notably, he also promoted an ecologically, culturally, and racially justified interpretation of the ideologically driven cultural pessimism of the Conservative Revolution, whose significance, if one adheres to the view of Fritz Stern, has frequently been underestimated in connection with the atrocities committed by the Germans.[1] Conservative Revolutionaries in the early twentieth century – toward whom many European neo-fascist intellectuals and agitators oriented themselves – repeatedly bemoaned the decline, deterioration, and destruction of culture and tradition, or, like Schultze-Naumburg, lamented changes and damage to the environment resulting from modernity (changes such as those brought on by urbanization and the indiscriminate use of space). These Conservative Revolutionaries, considered the forerunners

1. Fritz Stern, *Kulturpessimismus als politische Gefahr. Eine Analyse nationaler* *Ideologie in Deutschland* (Stuttgart: Klett-Cotta, 1963/2018).

of National Socialism, criticized liberal democracy for denying and dissolving the supposedly natural inequality of human groups. The National Socialists imposed this inequality through brute force.

Inequality was and is the core of right-wing extremism. Schultze-Naumburg wrote that it was a mistake for the working class to adopt "the false doctrine of the equality of individuals," because, in this worldview, nothing is less unequal than people, and this inequality cannot be redressed through external factors. In 1928, he wrote: "Selection with the aim of adaptation to the environment has thus far, unfortunately, rarely been implemented intentionally,"[2] thereby advocating extermination under ecological pretexts. Liberalism was the main enemy of the fascists, or at least on a par with socialism. Recurring cycles of antisemitism in Christian traditions served as a central ideological bridge and abetted the nationalist crusade.

Today as well, reactionaries continue to oppose equality and fairness, particularly with regards to race, gender, and class. The more apparent the insubstantiality of the pretenses for justifying inequality, the more aggressively and irrationally its proponents and beneficiaries insist on imposing it. Conspiracy narratives, which are frequently grounded in antisemitism, are an expression of this radicalization. Spatial imperialism, false theories about the biological basis of race, industrial extermination, and the Second World War are the result of such ideologies.

The authoritarian, nationalistic, and generally antisemitic struggle against modernity was, however, never a fight against using modern technology to advance one's own cause. From the Volksempfänger (the Nationalist Socialist-era "people's" radio) and the Volkswagen (the "people's" car) to the V2 rocket – as well as today's social media and artificial intelligence – fascist movements have always pioneered the exploitation of modern technologies for purposes of political agitation.

> "Fascist ecology is only ostensibly based
> on the notion that human beings and
> nature are one; in reality, it is rooted in
> the conviction that politics must imitate
> the ruthlessness of nature's dictum
> 'eat or be eaten.'"

The relationship between racism and social space in extreme right-wing thought, which also finds expression in aesthetic questions, represents a claim to hegemony based on brutality and the exercise of power. The simultaneity of, first, the romantic glorification of the environment and nature (in Hitler's case, mountains in particular), second, brute urban architecture intended to demonstrate power, and, third, the industrial rationality of human

2. Paul Schultze-Naumburg, *Kunst und Rasse* (Munich: J. F. Lehmann, 1928), p. 315.

extermination facilities and war production reveals what was truly intended: the domination of people and nature. This goal resonates in the National Socialist regime's claims to totality, aimed at replicating the alleged hierarchies of the natural world in human societies, enforced through extreme violence. Fascist ecology is only ostensibly based on the notion that human beings and nature are one; in reality, it is rooted in the conviction that politics must imitate the ruthlessness of nature's dictum "eat or be eaten" by harnessing the means of industrial technologies – rather than using these tools to improve living conditions for all.

In an era of rapidly escalating climate crisis, the voices of eco-fascism are growing ever louder. In the United States, New Zealand, and Germany, racial terrorists even justify their violence in eco-fascist terms, claiming that the number of non-white individuals must be reduced in order to save the white race and its "rightful" home. While such extreme voices are a minority, they point to a more widespread problem: attempting to cope with the escalating climate crisis without acknowledging or questioning one's own privileges.

Another problematic approach to global warming that still dominates anti-ecological discourses is the denial of its existence, of the contributing role played in it by human beings and industry, and our ability to influence it. Pseudoscientific studies, paid experts, fearmongering, disinformation, and the trivialization of climate change are significant facets of prevailing ideologies. Just as they once fought against democratization and industrialization, right-wing radicals today battle against both decarbonization and multiculturalism as the twin forces supposedly destroying their homeland, nation, economy, and culture. These narratives are revealing, since they, too, oppose changes that might be inconvenient, expensive, or disruptive, and that make the Global North aware of its responsibility for the consequences of industrialization – which those who have contributed the least suffer the most.

On a structural level, climate racism aims to obscure the ecological and social costs of the predominantly white West's industrial affluence at the expense of predominantly non-white regions and communities. Climate racism functions both as a framework and as a mechanism that reproduces and legitimizes these structures. As a global principle of inequality, climate racism shapes the reality of our daily lives; it is part of the everyday practice that binds us to all these structures. The consequences of carbon emissions and environmental damage caused by the extraction of raw materials are felt in particular by individuals who are already marginalized. Statistically, the people and regions affected most intensely by climate change today are poor, female, and BIPOC.

Every time we find a wind turbine aesthetically objectionable or are angered by a drinking straw made of paper, we should remind ourselves that the same system that imposes rules for environmentally friendly behavior on billions of people and makes energy and everyday necessities more expensive also enables just a few super-rich individuals to emit more carbon with their private jets, mega-yachts, and consumption of luxuries in one week than the average citizen does in his or her entire life. The super-rich emit thousands of times more greenhouse gasses than the average citizen. The richest ten percent are thus responsible for as much emissions as the poorest fifty percent of the world population. How can that be justified? Protecting the climate is not a question of adopting morally superior lifestyles, but rather of correcting social inequalities.

Nationalism is the counter-reaction to the polluter-pays principle. It is no coincidence that extreme right-wing, authoritarian, and fascist movements and parties have emerged in recent years in many countries with pasts and presents shaped by colonialism, industrialization, and high carbon emissions, whose elites in particular benefit from global inequalities. These movements and parties have at least one thing in common: they embrace ideologies that defend inequalities. This includes resistance to the emancipation of women and nonbinary individuals, the equal rights of migrants, robust protections for the environment and indigenous populations, critical race theory, and a true coming-to-terms with the past. It also entails the pursuit of policies that redistribute wealth and resources from the bottom to the top and deregulate financial markets, while simultaneously stoking culture wars that position the lower and middle classes as victims of globalist, green, elite, and supposedly woke "others." While these are the classes that are most affected by inequality, at the same time they often play a significant role in stabilizing regimes of extreme inequality.

"Without climate justice ...
a democratic future is inconceivable."

Without climate justice, however, a democratic future is inconceivable. To achieve this, the economies and design of cities, shared spaces, transportation, and food systems must change – but these changes need not impact all people to the same degree. If the individuals who bear the largest responsibility reduced their emissions to a more tolerable level, the lifestyles of the majority of people would barely need to change. (Broadly, though, we need to considerably reduce the space-wasting overconsumption of meat across the board.) Climate justice demands that the wealthy and powerful, the main contributors to global warming, use their advantages to protect the poor, weak, and disempowered from the destructive consequences of climate change. Every day, though, we see evidence that the biggest offenders will not change voluntarily – and some are willing to entertain fascism in order to defend their privileges. But by identifying the root causes, patterns, and ideologies that exist within our inequitable systems, we can chart paths toward climate justice and a more equitable world. For every emancipatory movement has only achieved progress against great resistance.

This text is based on the talk "Spaces and Ideologies of Inequality in the Climate Crisis" presented at dieDAS's walk + talk Symposium on September 2, 2023, as well as on the book by Matthias Quent, Christoph Richter, and Axel Salheiser, *Klimarassismus. Der Kampf der Rechten gegen die ökologische Wende* (Munich: Piper, 2022).

Sarah M. Whiting

Dean and Josep Lluís Sert Professor
of Architecture, Harvard University Graduate School of Design,
and dieDAS Advisory Council Member

Monumental Consistencies and Complexities

Germane Barnes's 2023 dieDAS curatorial theme, Monumental Affairs_Living with Contested Spaces, goes right to the heart of a challenge that the field of architecture has long faced: How can design capture and carry monumentality? If monuments are understood to be *repositories of collective memory*, as the Getty Research Institute claimed in their MONUMENTality exhibition of 2019, how might they navigate complex, nuanced, or disputed histories, personages, and spaces?

It's not a new dilemma. In 1937, cultural critic Lewis Mumford declared the "Death of the Monument," issuing its final rites in the pages of the British publication *CIRCLE*. Equating monuments with tombstones, or markers for something stable, concrete, and dead, and modernity with the realm of the living, the immediate, and the nomadic, Mumford concluded that "the very notion of a modern monument is a contradiction in terms: If it is a monument, it cannot be modern, and if it is modern, it cannot be a monument."[1]

Mumford's text, excerpted from his manuscript for *The Culture of Cities* (which would be published a year later, in 1938), formed part of his larger agenda to push society out of the "dead," "Paleotechnic" age of industrialization into what Mumford called – paying homage to Patrick Geddes – the "Biotechnic" age, a period of flexibility, liberation from the mechanical, and detachment from the physicality of the past.[2] For Mumford, the "Biotechnic" provided a means of combating the anomie of the capitalist metropolis by enabling a grassroots model of participatory democracy that foregrounded the individual who, Mumford believed, had been rendered invisible by the bureaucratization of the industrialized nation-state. Mumford's flexible, "organic bodies" of renewal depended on this very brink of anarchy for their force. Individualized anarchy, or the threat thereof, kept democracy from being annihilated by a capitalist bureaucrat and centralized government.

Operating from the same assumption that monumentality as we know it must be dead, recently arrived European émigrés Sigfried Giedion, Josep Lluís Sert, and Fernand Léger reached an entirely different conclusion in New York in 1943 when they collaborated on a response to a solicitation they had each received from the American Abstract Artists group asking them to contribute to an upcoming publication. Rather than bury monumentality, the three friends proposed its reformulation. Adopting an avant-gardist manifesto

1. Lewis Mumford, "The Death of the Monument," in John Leslie Martin, Ben Nicholson, and Naum Gabo, eds., *CIRCLE: International Survey of Constructive Art* (London: Faber and Faber, 1937; repr. 1971), 264.
2. Mumford thoughtfully provided his readers with a lexicon to explain these Geddesian neologisms; "PALEOTECHNIC: Refers to the coal and iron economy ...; NEOTECHNIC: Refers to the new economy ... based on the use of electricity, the lighter metals ... and rare metals; BIOTECHNIC: Refers to an emergent economy, already separating out from the neotechnic (purely mechanical) complex, and pointing to a civilization in which the biological sciences will be freely applied to technology, and in which technology itself will be oriented toward the culture of life.... In the biotechnic order the biological and social arts become dominant.... Improvements, instead of depending solely upon mechanical manipulations of matter and energy will rest upon a more organic utilization of the entire environment, in response to the needs of organisms and groups considered in their multifold relations: physical, biological, social; economic, esthetic, psychological." *The Culture of Cities* (New York: Harcourt Brace Jovanovich, 1938; repr. 1970), 495–96.

format, they produced the pithy, polemical "Nine Points on Monumentality," outlining a platform for a new form of monumentality within the context of US-American democratic society. Although the manifesto itself was not published until 1956 (in German; it was published in English in 1958), it formed the basis for Giedion's widely disseminated 1944 text "A Need for a New Monumentality" and was the basis for the eighth meeting of the Congrès Internationale d'Architecture Moderne (CIAM) in Hoddesdon, England, in 1951.

While Giedion, Léger, and Sert came to an opposite conclusion from Mumford, they shared Mumford's faith in flexibility, lightness, and mobility: "Mobile elements can constantly vary the aspect of the buildings. These mobile elements, changing positions and casting different shadows when acted upon by wind or machinery, can be the source of new architectural effects." And also like Mumford, for Giedion, Sert, and Léger, the operative term with which they concluded their polemic was freedom: "In such monumental layouts, architecture and city planning could attain a new freedom...." But whereas Mumford's freedom was the freedom of the individual from the constraints of mechanization, Giedion, Sert, and Léger's is the freedom of expression of "the collective force – the people."

For these three Europeans, in other words, the horrors of the war instilled a desire to recover or redeem collective expression. Giedion's focus was the question of collective subjectivity, that is, how aesthetic experience defines a collective sensibility. The assumption, never stated explicitly in the "Nine Points" text but glimpsed elsewhere, was that politics and economics would be engendered by a new aesthetics. In his "Need for a New Monumentality" text of 1944, for example, Giedion suggests that architecture could serve economist John Maynard Keynes's call for economic stimulation: "Why not keep the economic machinery going by creating civic centers?" Fitting the ethos of the war into the terms of aesthetics, Giedion, Sert, and Léger drew on the question of monumentality as a means of tapping into an already mature debate over modernism's capacity for expression.

Ultimately, then, what separated Mumford from Giedion was not so much a belief for or against monumentality – at the end of the day, both sides favored an architecture and urbanism that corresponded to the expression of each one's particular definition of the zeitgeist – but, rather, the differences underlying their conception of the modernist subject and the form of that subject's public sphere: Mumford's singular public subject participated in a collective experience of civic symbols, whereas Giedion's collective subjects engaged a public sphere of abstract symbolic form.

Today's zeitgeist has further challenged the very concept of monumentality. Complicating the mid-century debate over the possibility of civic symbolism affecting a singular or collective public subject, we now find ourselves in a world that questions former monuments and, further, that questions the assumptions that underlay former definitions of collective subjectivity. An article in the *Washington Post* specified that more than 140 Confederate monuments had been removed from public land in the United States between 2015 and 2021;[3] *The Guardian* wrote of almost seventy tributes to colonialists and slave traders that had been removed across the UK during a similar period;[4] and writing in *Politico*, historian Joshua Zeitz asserts that, "In 1949, the Federal Republic of Germany (West Germany) criminalized the display of swastikas; the symbol was also scraped and sometimes blown off of buildings. The federal state systematically destroyed statues and monuments, razed many Nazi architectural structures and buried executed military and civilian officials in mass, unmarked graves so that their resting grounds would not become Nazi shrines."[5]

    Such reassessments of monuments, of people, of histories have been taking place for decades now on various national stages across the world. It's also been a focus for many institutions, including Harvard University, which released the Report of the Presidential Committee on Harvard and the Legacy of Slavery in April of 2022, accompanying the announcement of the report with a commitment of $100 million to fund its recommendations. Among those recommendations was one advocating a memorial: "We recommend that the University recognize and honor the enslaved people whose labor facilitated the founding, growth, and evolution of Harvard through a permanent and imposing physical memorial, convening space, or both."[6]

    All to say, almost ninety years after Lewis Mumford declared monumentality's demise, we can say with confidence that it is anything but dead. Returning to Germane Barnes's call to action with Monumental Affairs_Living with Contested Spaces, the topic is at once timely and timeless. Like dieDAS, the GSD tackles this continuously complicated terrain by reading history with nuance, care, and depth, while also considering our future, by experimenting with materials, investigating resources, and exploring ways that people with diverse backgrounds can live and work together. The synergy of our two institutions is underscored by the number of GSD affiliates who have been dieDAS Fellows or participated in dieDAS's annual walk + talk Symposium. We look forward to further collaborations once the Architects' Wing is restored and becomes a site for further research.

    By 1949, Mumford grudgingly suggested that monumentality might best be replaced by messaging: "Perhaps the best way to restate Giedion's thesis would be to say that it is not enough for a modern building to be

3. Bonnie Berkowitz and Adrian Blanco, "A Record Number of Confederate Monuments Fell in 2020, but Hundreds Still Stand. Here's Where." *Washington Post*, updated March 12, 2021; https://www.washingtonpost.com/graphics/2020/national/confederate-monuments/ (accessed April 16, 2024)

4. Aamna Mohdin and Rhi Storer, "Tributes to Slave Traders and Colonists Removed across UK," *The Guardian*, January 29, 2021; https://www.theguardian.com/world/2021/jan/29/tributes-to-slave-traders-and-colonialists-removed-across-uk (accessed April 16, 2024).

5. Joshua Zeitz, "Why There Are No Nazi Statues in Germany: What the South Can Learn from Postwar Europe," *Politico*, August 20, 2017; https://www.politico.com/magazine/story/2017/08/20/why-there-are-no-nazi-statues-in-germany-215510/ (accessed April 16, 2024).

6. Recommendation: Honor Enslaved People through Memorialization, Research, Curricula, and Knowledge Dissemination," *Report of the Presidential Committee on Harvard and the Legacy of Slavery*, April 26, 2022; https://legacyofslavery.harvard.edu/report (accessed April 19, 2024).

something and do something: it must also say something ... Modern architects have mastered their grammar and vocabulary and are ready for speech."[7] Redesigned as a place for conversation, research, and production, dieDAS at Saaleck will have us all talking.

7. Lewis Mumford, "Monumentalism, Symbolism, and Style," *The Architectural Review* (April 1949): 173.

II. Saalecker Werkstätten

23

23. The dieDAS – Design Akademie Saaleck campus in Saxony-Anhalt, Germany, originally designed and built by Paul Schultze-Naumburg just after the turn of the 20th century

24

25. Egidio Marzona, Marzona Foundation Board of Directors
26. Andreas Silbersack, Marzona Foundation Board of Directors

27. Arne Cornelius Wasmuth, Marzona Foundation Board of Directors and dieDAS Founding Director
28. Tatjana Sprick, dieDAS Director of Program and Development

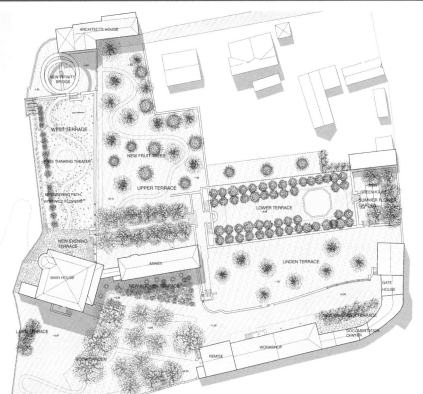

ARCHITECTS HOUSE

NEW INFINITY
BRIDGE

WEST TERRACE

NEW FRUIT TREES

"FREE THINKING THEATER"

UPPER TERRACE

"MEANDERING PATH"
"WITH WILD FLOWERS"

LOWER TERRACE

GREENHOUSE
SUMMER FLOWER
GARDEN

NEW EVENING
TERRACE

ANNEX

LINDEN TERRACE

MAIN HOUSE

NEW KITCHEN TERRACE

GATE
HOUSE

LAWN TERRACE

NEW LAVENDER TERRACE

DOCUMENTATION
CENTER

ROCK GARDEN

REMISE

WORKSHOP

29. Dorte Mandrup's site plan design for the Saalecker Werkstätten

30. Dorte Mandrup's rendering of the adaptive reuse of the Saalecker Werkstätten
31. Dorte Mandrup's design for an Infinity Bridge to connect the Saalecker Werkstätten and the gardens

32. Dorte Mandrup's rendering of the adaptive reuse of the Saalecker Werkstätten

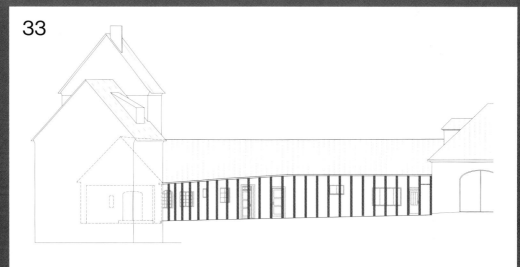

33

■ DEMOLITION

■ NEW CONSTRUCTION

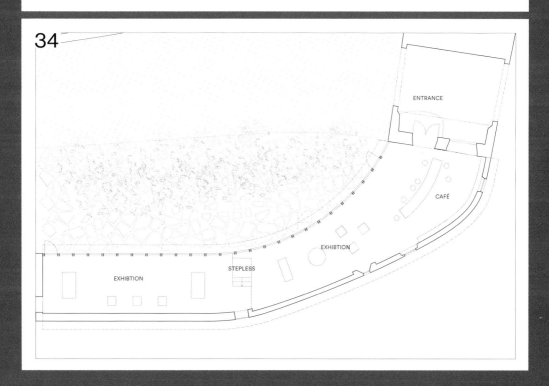

34

ENTRANCE

CAFÉ

EXHIBITION

EXHIBTION

STEPLESS

Prof. Dr.-Ing.

Daniela Spiegel

Professor of Heritage Conservation and Architectural History, Bauhaus-Universität Weimar

The Making of an Uncomfortable Monument

Over the past decades, more and more monuments have been declared controversial in public discourse. In the meantime, "uncomfortable monuments" have become a separate branch of research in monument theory. But what exactly are uncomfortable monuments?

When approaching the question, it helps to first take a closer look at the terminology. According to the etymological origin of the word (from the Latin *monere*, meaning to remember or to draw attention to something), monuments are objects that remind us today, in the present, of something from the past. If the objects were created specifically for this reminiscent purpose, such as statues, they are referred to as *intentional monuments*. However, there are also so-called *unintentional monuments*, which act as material witnesses to something that is deemed worth remembering and are subsequently declared monuments. A monument is therefore a carrier of values, and identifying and explaining these values is a core task of monument preservation. The classic values that in Germany are laid down in the federal monument protection laws include, for example, the worthiness of preservation for historical and artistic reasons as well as for urban planning, technical, or ethnographic reasons.

35.
Advertisement for the Saalecker Werkstätten, ca. 1920

While most of the aforementioned values have positive connotations, such as outstanding achievements in the respective field, the historical value of an object can also refer to a negative event or person. Moreover, the value attributions are dependent on social dynamics and are therefore not static. This works in both directions: formerly discredited buildings can be appreciated again by the next generation, and conversely, people or events that have been memorialized or commemorated can be judged adversely by later generations.

The latter was and still is a central issue in the area of intentional monuments. A change in perspective or a questioning of the previous culture of remembrance can suddenly make such monuments uncomfortable – sometimes so uncomfortable that they are toppled or removed from their pedestals. The appropriate or "correct" way of dealing with them is usually the subject of heated debate; monuments are therefore often objects of sensitive social negotiation processes.

In the field of unintentional monuments, the term "uncomfortable" is applicable in multiple contexts. For example, it is used for younger buildings that have already been recognized as monuments by experts, without enlisting a social consensus. Such monuments are usually only uncomfortable for a period of around thirty years, until they are sufficiently historicized and thus generally accepted.

In other instances, the term is used for heritage sites where there is a social consensus on their preservation, but which are uncomfortable due to their history, such as places of crime. However, the term "uncomfortable" sometimes seems too weak for these types of monuments; some places are downright *contaminated* by their history, so that no other use than as a museum or place of learning seems possible.

However, the most challenging sites or objects to navigate in terms of monument preservation are those where the discomfort is not superficially visible and where a use other than as a commemorating place or memorial may be possible and/or sensible. Finding an appropriate function for these locales that also actively deals with their fraught history is always a major challenge. And it becomes really uncomfortable when there is a strong discrepancy between the uncomfortable legacy and the comfortable form that surrounds it.

36.
Paul Schultze-Naumburg

The latter undoubtedly includes the Saalecker Werkstätten, which Paul Schultze-Naumburg (1869–1949) created at the beginning of the twentieth century as his own home and soon also his company headquarters. The extensive ensemble is fantastically situated: the site's structures rise boldly on the rocky mountain cliff above the Saale River bend, with a wide view of the hilly landscape, shielded to the east by a wing of farm buildings that leads in an elegant sweep to the towering gatehouse, with staggered gardens on several terraces in between.

Although it has been empty for decades, the place still exudes the pleasant tranquility of a refuge where it is conceivably easy, even pleasant, to live and work. In short, the place itself actually seems very comfortable at first glance. Moreover, no terrible physical violence took place here (at least that we know of), and the buildings, interiors, and garden designs that were created in the local workshops were also quite common products for the upper and middle classes of the time.

37.
The Saalecker Werkstätten

It is the resident mastermind, an autodidactic architect who personally designed and created the place and all its details, who imbues the Saalecker Werkstätten with an uncomfortable legacy. Schultze-Naumburg is indeed one of the most intriguing and irritating personalities in German cultural history of the first half of the twentieth century. At the beginning of his career, he was certainly a supporter of reformist tendencies. He was one of the cofounders of the Deutscher Werkbund, which advocated modern product design, and was a founding member of the Deutscher Bund Heimatschutz (German Confederation of Homeland Security). He criticized the excesses of industrialization and historicism above all in the *Kulturarbeiten* series published between 1901 and 1917, with which he became a pioneer of the concept of the cultural landscape that is still important today. After the First World War, however, the conservative reformer became a fervent supporter of racist National Socialist cultural policy and fought against the artistic avant-garde of modernism. Schultze-Naumburg's aesthetic and political radicalization culminated in 1928 with the publication of the book *Kunst und Rasse* (Art and Race), in which he anticipated the discrediting arguments of National Socialism's so-called "degenerate art." As early as the nineteen-twenties, Hitler, Goebbels, and Himmler were welcome guests in Saaleck, and Schultze-Naumburg himself became a member of the National

Socialist German Workers' Party (NSDAP), more commonly known as the Nazi Party, in 1930.

The Saalecker Werkstätten were therefore created by a person who not only shared the racist, National Socialist ideology, but also actively participated in its theoretical foundation – a form of violence in its own right. He formulated, discussed, and wrote down his thoughts in this very place – in the study, at the dining table, on the terrace. This is what gives the site, a place of perpetrators, its uncomfortable legacy.

Schultze-Naumburg only worked in Saaleck until 1930, when the Nazi party moved into the Thuringian state government and appointed him director of the United Arts Academy in Weimar. In this role, he saw it as his task to turn the school back into a training center for "true" German architecture after the "aberrations of the Bauhaus." This directorship, which lasted barely ten years, is in turn an uncomfortable legacy for those of us connected to today's Bauhaus-Universität Weimar, where I have the privilege to teach and research. Schultze-Naumburg is a firm link between Weimar and Saaleck, not only in the past, but also in the present.

The positive turnaround that the Saalecker Werkstätten experienced after decades of vacancy began at a conference that Hans-Rudolf Meier and I organized through the Chair of Heritage Conservation and Architectural History at the Bauhaus-Universität Weimar in December 2015. There, a semester project was presented, in which students of urban studies and architecture dealt with various aspects of Schultze-Naumburg's controversial and uncomfortable legacy and the then vacant ensemble in Saaleck – and highlighted possible usage perspectives.

38.
Arne Cornelius Wasmuth speaks to visitors at dieDAS Open House 2022

One of the interested conference participants was Arne Cornelius Wasmuth, who, rightly inspired, subsequently took on the site with incredible verve. Thanks to him, the Marzona Foundation, and the dieDAS concept they initiated – as well as the dedicated team with whom they collaborate – a new function was found for the property that not only preserves the architectural heritage in a manner appropriate to a listed building, but also actively addresses the uncomfortable content of the heritage and makes it usable for society in a beneficial way.

Stephan Kujas

Heritage Expert
and Monument Conservator, Stadt Weißenfels

The Transformation of an Uncomfortable Monument

The small village of Saaleck is located near the city of Naumburg in the Saale River valley in central Germany, in an area long known for wine cultivation and agriculture. In the alluring landscape of this region, an architectural ensemble, including a stately country house and garden, was constructed just after the turn of the twentieth century on a cliff towering above the valley and beneath the ruins of a medieval castle. The complex was erected by the painter, self-taught architect, racist ideologue, and nationalist mastermind Paul Schultze-Naumburg (1869–1949), who had his residence and the headquarters of his successful architecture, landscaping, and interior design firm, the Saalecker Werkstätten (Saaleck Workshops), here between 1903 and 1930.

39.
The Saalecker Werkstätten

During his time in Saaleck, Schultze-Naumburg wrote a series of much-read treatises on art, architecture, taste, and observations of nature, titled *Kulturarbeiten* (Cultural Works). His 1928 book *Kunst und Rasse* (Art and Race), based on his notions of a nationalistic art and intended first and foremost to defame modern art as "degenerate," achieved dubious renown. In the juxtapositions of pictures in the book, he positioned works of modernism opposite photographs of individuals with disabilities and deformities to support his assertions. Through the denigration of individuals and artworks, he thus helped to lay the foundations for the subsequent murderous developments in National Socialist Germany.

In the nineteen-twenties, an informal circle of infamous National Socialists – including Adolf Hitler, Joseph Goebbels, and Heinrich Himmler – formed in Saaleck around Paul Schultze-Naumburg, regarding him as an important channel for gaining access to the German bourgeoisie. As a result of his journalistic reach, personal networks, and popularity with the middle-class public, Schultze-Naumburg contributed significantly to lending the racist ideology a respectable veneer and making it acceptable to the masses. With his work and influence, he was thus an early trailblazer for National Socialism.

As a site connected with National Socialist intellectual history, the complex of the Saalecker Werkstätten is today an "uncomfortable monument" that will always bear the imprint of its dark history. At first glance, however, the house and garden in Saaleck reveal nothing of the racist and antisemitic ideology that was formulated there. The past lies hidden and is not readily discernible for visitors. This is why a differentiated examination of the site with respect to monument protection and content must take place in order to elucidate this background and make it accessible. The Marzona Stiftung Neue Saalecker Werkstätten is currently addressing this task.

In 2018, the Berlin-based art collector and patron Egidio Marzona acquired the country house and garden of the former Saalecker Werkstätten through the Marzona Stiftung with the aim of creating a progressive learning center for designers and architects to conduct research regarding approaches for a better, more egalitarian, and more sustainable future while at the same time promoting discourse on the history of the location.

Marzona formulated the mission of the foundation as follows: "In this place, where we will remember the darkest chapter of our history, we will use free exchange to push back against the damage wrought by far-right populism; we will be an international, liberal breeding-ground for innovative ideas." With the conversion of the Saalecker Werkstätten for new, productive uses, the foundation intentionally focuses on the uncomfortable monument so as to set a clear and palpable symbol of the forces for change in a democratic and open society.

Thanks to the support of the State of Saxony-Anhalt and the Federal Government's Ministry of Culture and Media, preparations for the rehabilitation and conversion of the complex for dieDAS – Design Akademie Saaleck have been underway since 2019. In addition to numerous preliminary examinations, the Landesamt für Denkmalpflege und Archäologie (State Office for Conservation and Archeology) of Saxony-Anhalt first elaborated monument-protection objectives to serve as a guideline for further planning. A total restoration and reconstruction of the complex in Saaleck in line with the ideas of Schultze-Naumburg, however, was never considered.

40.
Arne Cornelius Wasmuth and Egidio Marzona at dieDAS Open House 2022

Since the Marzona Stiftung distances itself from the original builder and his ideas, the redesign of the site of the Saalecker Werkstätten and its contemporary valorization are being given a forward-looking design expression.

To this end, a limited international competition was held in 2020 in order to obtain proposals for the rehabilitation and reorientation of the site through the use of a homogeneous architectural language for all the new building elements, and, simultaneously, to formulate a suitable approach to the existing complex and its layers of history. Since its construction, the site has been modified and redesigned several times, and the still-extant traces of development are to be preserved – at least in part. Danish architect Dorte Mandrup's ideas for the complex as a whole prevailed in a juried selection process. The winning design makes the past visible up to recent times while simultaneously adding a contemporary skin of new materials and colors to enable future content, ideas, and visions.

41.
Visitors exploring the media station at dieDAS Open House 2022

An important component of the work of the Marzona Stiftung is the establishment of a learning and documentation center for examining the antisemitic and National Socialist history of the site and its architect's difficult legacy. The center will be located near the gatehouse and, when completed, open for visitors on an ongoing basis. A scholarly reappraisal will take place in parallel with the planned construction work, and its results will lead to an analogue and digital exhibition concept. The future exhibition is intended to make a reflective approach to the past productive for political education today by referring to various contemporary political and cultural issues. On behalf of the foundation, the Zentrum für Antisemitismusforschung (ZfA, Center for Research on Antisemitism) at the Technische Universität Berlin has already created an initial concept sketch for the permanent exhibition, and work is currently underway to implement it in the next stages.

A media station illustrating Schultze-Naumburg's antisemitic networks that was originally exhibited at the Topography of Terror documentation center in Berlin is now on loan to Saaleck, where it is currently on view. This media station is one result of the Deutsche Forschungsgemeinschaft's (DFG, German Research Foundation) collaborative project "Paul Schultze-Naumburg and the Aesthetics of Folkishness (Volkstum) in Architecture and Garden Culture" of the Universität der Künste in Berlin and the Technische Universität Darmstadt. In order to make the findings from this DFG project usable for the learning and documentation center, a joint collaboration is currently being prepared with the lead researchers, the ZfA, the Landeszentrale für politische Bildung (Regional Center for Political Education), and the Institut für Landesgeschichte Sachsen-Anhalt (Institute for the Regional History of Saxony-Anhalt). The results of the accompanying research will be gradually implemented in the development of the exhibition and innovative communication formats.

Another component of the foundation's activities will be an artistic examination of the site as an uncomfortable monument. This will make it possible to experience individual perspectives and experiences connected to the history of the Saalecker Werkstätten as well as the perspectives of international artists.

42.
Prof. Hans-Rudolf Meier lectures on the life and legacy of Paul Schultze-Naumburg at dieDAS Open House 2022

For the Marzona Stiftung, the site of the former Saalecker Werkstätten represents a challenging legacy that must, nonetheless, be approached with open eyes and clear objectives. The foundation's path to reclaiming and redesigning the site will be an ongoing process that unfolds and develops through the various protagonists involved with it. In this way, the Saalecker Werkstätten will be transformed into a dynamic and inclusive location for free thought, design, discourse, and artistic expression that is both historically responsible and future-oriented.

Dorte Mandrup

Architect and Founder and Creative Director of Dorte Mandrup

Exposing, Leaving, Adding

How do you insert new meaning into an otherwise uncomfortable monument without simultaneously erasing the past? Finding the balance is an extremely complicated task. It requires a precise and careful reading of the place, its history, and the emotional meaning it carries in order to make strategic, sensitive interventions that allow future generations to engage with this history, without letting it interfere with the development of new movements and values. Our task as architects is to find a way to instill newfound positivity by commenting on the past, exposing it, and taking away its power – making it harmless.

43.
Layers of history inside the Saalecker Werkstätten

Nestled on a cliff above the Saale River, the Saalecker Werkstätten look back on a grave and complex past, irrevocably tied to architect and racist ideologue Paul Schultze-Naumburg, who would become known as one of the leading proponents of Nazi cultural policy. In the mid-nineteen-twenties, the complex of buildings – otherwise relatively neutral spaces set in the beautiful, sloping landscape – became a plateau for National Socialist sentiment and ultimately a think tank for totalitarian and racist ideology. The site holds a difficult and disturbing history that can neither be ignored and forgotten, nor allowed to define or paralyze the creativity and ideals of future generations.

"It is the sum of all our memories that constitutes our understanding of the world and its existence."

It is the sum of all our memories that constitutes our understanding of the world and its existence. It grants us the ability to relate to time and space. Buildings and landscapes record the past in different ways. Sometimes in tangible elements or visible traces of physical activity. Sometimes in stories passed on through generations. The memories accumulate and are preserved within the layers of the built fabric. Monuments and relics inform our collective identity and help us recall decisive moments in history. However, this process is not static. The past is in a reciprocal relationship with the present; the meanings we add to our buildings are there to define the past, the present, and future.

Preserving and understanding the physical evidence of the past, no matter how uncomfortable it may be, is part of developing an evolving society towards a better future. By allowing the past to coexist with the present, we accept that our presence in time, the values and content of our society, depends on our actions now.

The Saalecker Werkstätten are not a static place either. The buildings have transformed several times since they were built in the beginning of the twentieth century. First established in 1904 as a community for reform-oriented architects and artists, it now lies in the shadows of the political radicalization of Paul Schultze-Naumburg. The architectural expression of the first building of the Saalecker Werkstätten complex has a clear connection to the Vienna Secession, Vienna Werkbund, and Deutscher Werkbund, and thereby reflects aesthetic ideals found in other places in Europe at the time. It does not specifically reveal disturbing ideals or allude to the horror that was to come.

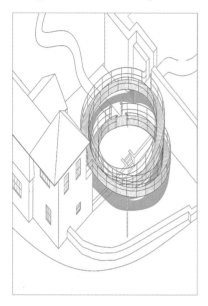

44.
Dorte Mandrup's design for the Saalecker Werkstätten Infinity Bridge

Our approach to the transformation of the Saalecker Werkstätten is to create depth in the legibility of time, allowing the buildings to be understood from multiple perspectives, not only the dark period of the Nazi regime. Though there is very little documentation of the history of the buildings throughout the last sixty years, the traces from this period still hold significance both in forming an adequate understanding of the built fabric, and for the local community. While carefully restoring elements of the existing buildings, some parts are left untouched to reveal and reflect its varied content after the Schultze-Naumburg family moved away, and a new layer is added through a series of minimal yet forceful interventions bringing new values and content to the site.

In some places, we are reestablishing historical features that are important for the future spatial experience and wellbeing of inhabitants. This includes deliberately reestablishing old window openings to allow more daylight into the building and create a brighter atmosphere. Color is used as a didactic tool to create a tangible legibility of time through a composition of layers instead of a uniform surface. Some colors are restored according to the color archaeology, and some are left untouched. A third layer is added with new colors from a palette relating to the design ideas present around Europe when the Saalecker Werkstätten were built to convey an impression of what might have been. Luminous hues of red and yellow mark the few places where significant changes have been made within the building structure.

Inserting new content and meaning in charged places requires not only new functionality but also a representation of new ideals. We have therefore designed two types of interventions: one accommodating new functionality and one representing new ideals of diversity and free thinking. Since content and function can change with time, these interventions are designed to be moved, taken down, or added somewhere else. The garden was originally laid out symmetrically along two intersecting axes, underlining a strict movement. Adding a new layer of meandering paths, we are creating new ways of walking through the landscape, inspiring people to find alternative routes and discover new ways of using the garden. Towards the eastern corner of the garden, a new addition – the infinity bridge – interrupts the old axis, a symbolic gesture that creates multiple routes instead of one linear path.

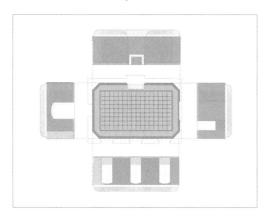

45.
Dorte Mandrup's design for the dining room, unfolded

By bridging the past and the present through an intricate composition of layers, the Saalecker Werkstätten become a place for reflection and education simultaneously. The idea of layering is not new. It is the way that historical buildings and landscapes have gradually transformed into what we see today, with great diversity of typologies, scales, and functions. By allowing historical structures to be inhabited by new functions, new values, and new content, we let history live and develop, hereby creating a richer and more complex understanding of our past and present. Transforming the Saalecker Werkstätten into a place for global design exchange and the open and democratic examination of art and design is thus a reminder of how impactful architecture can be.

III. Design Akademie Saaleck

46. The Saalecker Werkstätten during the debut dieDAS Fellowship Program in 2020

47. The debut dieDAS Fellowship Program 2020, Farming Materials' Ecologies: (left to right) Fellow Sasson Rafailov, Fellow Basse Stittgen, Fellow Svenja Keune, Fellow Talin Hazbar, Founding Director Arne Cornelius Wasmuth, Director of Program & Development Tatjana Sprick, and Artistic Director Maurizio Montalti

48. dieDAS Fellowship Program 2021, Symbiotic Habitat: (back to front) Director of Program & Development Tatjana Sprick, Artistic Director Maurizio Montalti, Founding Director Arne Cornelius Wasmuth, Head Mentor Eugenia Morpurgo, and Fellows Pollyanna Moss, Daniel Tish, Zeno Franchini, and Carolina Pacheco

49. dieDAS Fellowship Program 2021, Symbiotic Habitat: Fellows Pollyanna Moss and Daniel Tish working with mycelium

50. dieDAS Fellowship Program 2021, Symbiotic Habitat: willow and mycelium architectural sculpture built
    by the 2021 fellows

51. dieDAS Fellowship Program 2022, Designing Metabolic Relations: (back row, from left) Director of Program & Development Tatjana Sprick, Artistic Director Maurizio Montalti, and Founding Director Arne Cornelius Wasmuth, along with (in front row, from left) workshop leader Lili Carr of Feral Atlas, Head Mentor Eugenia Morpurgo, and Fellows Steffie de Gaetano, Giulia Pompilj, Adrian Pepe, and Nico Alexandroff

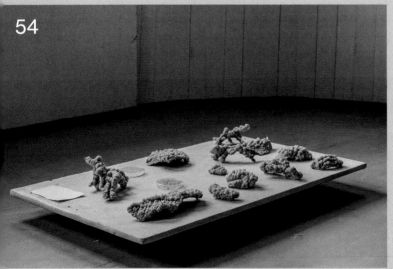

52. Wildrausch and local food cooking workshop during the dieDAS Fellowship Program 2022
53. dieDAS 2022 Fellows exhibit experiments with locally sourced pigments at the exhibition
    In/un becoming during the walk + talk Symposium 2022
54. dieDAS 2022 Fellows exhibit experiments with salt from Salina Bad Kösen at the exhibition
    In/un becoming during the walk + talk Symposium 2022

55. Architect Ronald Rael and design critic Alice Rawsthorn speak at the dieDAS walk + talk Symposium 2022, Designing Metabolic Relations

56. Design critic Alice Rawsthorn speaks at the dieDAS walk + talk Symposium 2022, Designing Metabolic Relations

57. Common lunch at the dieDAS walk + talk Symposium 2023, Monumental Affairs

58. dieDAS Open House 2023
59. Patron Ole M. Wasmuth with participants of the dieDAS 2022 Fellowship Program

60. dieDAS Patrons Lunch at Saalecker Werkstätten with Anna Engelhorn, 2021

dieDAS
Oral Histories

As dieDASdoc's inaugural publication, *Monumental Affairs_Living with Contested Spaces* brings a first opportunity to document in print the young institution's programmatic vision and approach, achievements to date, and future plans.

What follows is a series of interviews with boots-on-the-ground team members and collaborators who have played a key role in bringing dieDAS's mission to life. These interviews were conducted January–March 2024.

Tatjana Sprick

dieDAS Director of Program and Development
(2019–present)

As director of program and development, Tatjana Sprick is responsible for overseeing the planning and execution of dieDAS programs, including the fellowship program and walk + talk Symposium, as well as for helping the institution to build strong networks of collaborators, contributors, and supporters while maintaining engagement with the latest discourse around concepts for future living.

Prior to joining the dieDAS team in 2019, Sprick specialized in advising and consulting for international brands and institutions across the creative spectrum on the development of products, relationships, and experiences. She was responsible for initiating the design website L'ArcoBaleno and has advised and collaborated with clients such as the Fashion Council Germany, Yohji Yamamoto, Bikini Berlin, Dr. Hauschka, Elitis, and The DO School, as well as the multipurpose co-retail space ALHAMBRA BERLIN.

61.
Tatjana Sprick with Hans Albrecht Zieger, Winzervereinigung Freyburg, at dieDAS Open House 2022

When did you join the dieDAS team, and what is your role in the organization?

It was my good fortune to meet and get to know dieDAS's cofounder and director Arne Cornelius Wasmuth in 2018, just as the vision for the Marzona Foundation began to be realized. In the crucial months before, Arne had discovered that the historic residence and workspace of Paul Schultze-Naumburg was on the market and, soon after, confirmed the opportunity to transform the property, thanks to the generosity of collector and patron Egidio Marzona. The Marzona Stiftung was founded in October of 2018 by Egidio and Arne together with politician Andreas Silbersack. From the very beginning, I was eager to play a role, particularly with regards to content creation and programs.

It took us until early 2019 to fully formulate the foundation's structure and objectives and to outline the required roles. In September that year, we gathered a group of respected architecture and design experts and practitioners from around the world to share with them with the fundamental concept: a yearly in-residence fellowship program for multidisciplinary creatives in the fields of architecture, design, and craft alongside a permanent learning center focused on the history of the site. Over that three-day event, we discussed the programmatic goals, the legacy of the site and its architect, and our short- and long-term vision. With their feedback, we finalized our plans.

We established the dieDAS – Design Akademie Saaleck in the autumn of 2019, and I assumed the role of director of program and development.

What made you want to work with dieDAS?

The unique opportunity to shape and influence the development of an architectural and design curriculum for a fellowship program was extremely attractive. I am very grateful to have had the chance to contribute to the program's origins and to collaborate with our first artistic director, Maurizio Montalti, who suggested the structure for the program that we still follow today.

How would you define the overarching vision for dieDAS?

DieDAS is envisioned as a safe learning space for designers and architects who are dedicated to building a more egalitarian, sustainable, inclusive, and interconnected future. We raise and nurture new questions around the humane practice of architecture and design, always with respect for the connections that tie together yesterday, today, and tomorrow. Our motto is "Gestaltung mit Haltung," which can be translated to "design with attitude" or, perhaps more appropriately in our case, "design for a pluriverse world."

62.
Designer Julia Lohmann leads a workshop on algae and salt for the dieDAS Fellowship Program 2022

What are the key components and objectives of the fellowship program, and how does it work?

The fellowship program aims to empower, enable, and enlarge the next generation of leading creatives in the field of architecture and design. We are committed to offering emerging talents a unique set of experiences, collaborators, and resources to help them develop the innovative and socially conscious processes that are urgently needed to secure a better tomorrow.

The process begins with our artistic director. For this crucial position, we look for talented practitioners working at the frontiers of their fields to forge socially responsible approaches to addressing urgent issues, such as sustainability and equity and inclusion. During their two-year tenures at dieDAS, we give our artistic directors – to date, Maurizio Montalti (2020–22) and Germane Barnes (2023–24) – complete creative freedom to shape the fellowship curriculum and choose the annual theme.

Each year, our fellows are chosen through an invitation-only selection process. With the help of recommendations from esteemed professionals around the world, we identify potential candidates who have demonstrated high-caliber research and production, particularly in relation to the annual theme. We then send out a call to apply. Once the applications are in, our rotating selection committee narrows the candidates down to eight – each of whom are personally interviewed by the artistic director, who then selects the final four fellows.

During their residency at the dieDAS campus, the four annual fellows follow a carefully planned course tailored to their needs and to the artistic director's theme. They are provided with creative orientation, professional advice, workspaces, and support by internationally accomplished designers and architects who join digitally or physically in Saaleck. They are also asked to engage with the historical context of the site. At the end of the program, the fellows create an exhibition of the work they accomplished together, which is shared with a broader international audience during our annual walk + talk Symposium.

This curriculum is intended to give young architects and designers the opportunity to reflect on, question, and hopefully supplement their knowledge and practices through the lens of a specific theme. We strive to create a space for them that is free from prejudices and entrenched ways of thinking in order to interrogate the status quo, facilitate open exchange between a selected group of international fellows and mentors. A key component is the intensity of the time spent together in such a remote region, surrounded by beautiful nature as well as the uncomfortable history of the space.

As the historic buildings onsite are yet to be restored, our current fellowship program is more limited than what we hope to do in the future. After restoration, dieDAS will annually offer up to sixteen international fellowships for a duration of up to four months.

What is the broader objective of the walk + talk Symposium?
Each autumn, at the end of the fellowship program, dieDAS hosts an annual walk + talk weekend, offering transdisciplinary symposia in and around the campus exploring the annual theme. During these three days, guests from Germany and abroad are invited to connect and exchange views on relevant questions in the field of design, craft, and architecture. The fellows have the opportunity to show their practice to a global community while also contributing to the discourse. Our guests' collaboration, contributions, and support are invaluable to dieDAS and our fellows' ongoing development.

What other standout accomplishments should be mentioned?

I am very pleased to share a few great moments from the past few years. Our first off-site exhibition was presented at Design Miami/ Basel 2021. The installation included objects designed by 2020 and 2021 Fellows, curated by our artistic director Maurizio Montalti.

Another outstanding moment was when Basse Stittgen, a fellow from our debut program, was invited to participate in the PIN Auction at the Pinakothek der Moderne in November 2022.

Lastly, I'll also mention how special it was to present "Monument Masterclass," a panel discussion for students led by our 2023 Artistic Director Germane Barnes at Design Miami/ 2023.

63.
dieDAS 2021 Fellows exhibit at
Design Miami/ Basel in June 2021

How does dieDAS engage the surrounding community in Saxony-Anhalt?

This is an important aspect of our mission that will expand over time, particularly once the site renovations are completed. To date, we have been forging partnerships with nearby schools and universities in Halle and Weimar through student workshops, performances, and exhibitions as well through the local professors who serve as mentors for the fellowship program and speakers for the walk +talk Symposia.

In addition, once a year in spring or early summer, dieDAS invites the public to visit our campus and attend our open house. This event brings between 300 and 400 attendees each year and gives us the opportunity to connect with our neighbors and the broader regional community while sharing the dieDAS story with them. The event also helps us to connect and collaborate with German institutions and universities, such as Burg Halle and Bauhaus University.

What should we expect from dieDAS in the next five years? What about in the next twenty years?

Once Dorte Mandrup's architectural plan has been built — hopefully in 2027 — the ways we can use the campus and the programs we organize will grow immensely. Each year, we will dedicate the summer months to the fellowship program and walk + talk Symposium. The remaining eight months will be dedicated to hosting public and private events along with lectures and workshops in partnership with institutions and companies, including Harvard University Graduate School of Design. The site will include a permanent café, show kitchen, library, and learning facilities that will be available not only to our fellows and contributors but also to locals, tourists, and researchers.

We are currently focused on developing the vision for dieDAS doku, our forthcoming documentation center. Open to the public and accompanied by a strong digital component, the center will offer resources to learn about and engage the history of the site and its architect, alongside local history, genealogies, and racism and democracy studies. Produced in collaboration with scientists and designers, an on-site, interactive media station will illustrate the site's history and its relationship with democratic values. In addition, we're developing dieDAS art, a program dedicated to hosting contemporary art exhibitions in different spaces out in the surrounding community. Our first project presents the work of artists Ulla von Brandenburg and Olaf Holzapfel, curated by Daniel Marzona. It will open June 15, 2024, at the abandoned Kurhaus Bad Kösen in Naumburg (Saale).

64.
Arne Cornelius Wasmuth and Tatjana Sprick at the first dieDAS walk + talk Symposium in 2019

In the next twenty years, dieDAS has the potential to enlarge the campus and its offerings even further to engage even larger audiences. Overall, the future of dieDAS looks bright. We will continue to invest in industry-leading research and development while ensuring our platform continues to champion anti-racist, globally mindful perspectives and facilitate productive cross-cultural, interdisciplinary exchanges among diverse fellows, professionals, institutions, and companies. We believe these efforts cumulatively serve as a compelling testament to the power of change, community, and vision.

Maurizio Montalti

dieDAS inaugural Artistic Director (2020–22)

As dieDAS's inaugural artistic director, Italian designer Maurizio Montalti helped conceive the dieDAS fellowship program and created a pedagogical framework that would lay the groundwork for years to come. In this role, he sowed the seeds for future programs to build upon, taking the first steps in transforming a complex site with a dark history into a place for creative research, production, and discourse. Throughout his tenure, Montalti centered the interconnected nature of human and nonhuman entities in our shared ecosystem.

In addition to his academic work, Montalti is a biomaterials expert and a pioneer in the experimental field of fungal mycelium–based technologies. He critically explores contemporary material culture while cocreating with nature at every turn. Working at the intersection of design and biotech, he is founder of multidisciplinary studio Officina Corpuscoli as well as cofounder and chief mycelium officer (R&D director) at SQIM, a biomaterials company championing two brands — mogu and ephea™ — that craft biomaterials-based products for everyday use in sectors ranging from interior design and architecture to fashion.

65.
Artistic Director Maurizio Montalti at the 2020 Mycelium workshop

When did you join the dieDAS team? And what was your role?
I was first introduced to dieDAS in September 2019 during a symposium organized by the recently founded, but not yet launched dieDAS — instigated by a group that included Founding Director Arne Cornelius Wasmuth; Director of Program and Development Tatjana Sprick; and Egidio Marzona of the Marzona Foundation, the academy's benefactor. The event allowed the new organization to share its intentions with a small group of relevant creatives and educators, while also drawing on attendees' own experiences. Nothing was yet formalized, but they had a strong vision. I was a very active participant in the various brainstorming activities and workshops — so much so, apparently, that I was invited afterwards to join forces as the artistic director for the program. I embraced this privilege with open arms, and that's where the adventure began. I served as artistic director for the debut 2020 Fellowship and the two following years as well, where I had the opportunity to involve and work in close synergy with Head Mentor Eugenia Morpurgo.

What made you want to work with dieDAS?

I was excited by the vision and the opportunity to create a novel platform, something that differed from fellowship and residency programs that already existed. I've had enriching experiences myself elsewhere as a fellow in the past. I thought it could be interesting to take the best aspects from all these experiences, and to assess the functioning of various programs as we built our own.

We were starting with a completely blank canvas, so to speak – there were a lot of unknowns, including even how the physical space, which was not designed for a program like ours, would develop – and while that was daunting in some respects, it also offered a lot of opportunities. Rather than the usual top-down, vertical pyramid structure, for example, there was a wish to create a program based on functions and roles and collaboration. In this way, we could bring to life, even in our pedagogical structure, some of the values that dieDAS is based on – specifically, inclusivity and the capacity to welcome open, constructive dialogue among practitioners from different disciplines and backgrounds. The idea of helping to create a platform that could positively contribute to the expansion of critical discourse – especially around issues that are very dear to me: namely, social and environmental justice – was very seductive.

"I believe the vision of dieDAS is to create a space for creative encounters and the collision of ideas."

Being tasked to do that in this challenging geographical location was also intriguing. The location, while undeniably difficult for many reasons, was interesting from the point of view of the seclusion that it could offer and the history of the broader region as well – which, approximately 100 years earlier, saw the emergence of the Bauhaus movement. The idea of being able to contribute to the creation of a new movement approximately a century later that could positively impact the design field and creative discourse at large was one of the main drivers in my decision to join.

You touched a bit on some of the key values of dieDAS. How would you define the overarching vision and key objectives for the fellowship program itself?

I believe the vision of dieDAS is to create a space for creative encounters and the collision of ideas. To do so, we encourage creative production, informed by critical investigations with expert practitioners – primarily, at first, from the fields of design and architecture, and then later craft and beyond. The idea was to put together people from different backgrounds – creative, educational, cultural, and more – and see what kind of insight we could generate from their possibly positive collisions and the related exchanges. And we had the luxury to do so without the need for establishing the traditional KPIs and so on; both the organization and I approached the program as an experiment, an adventure rooted in a learning-by-doing approach. It was very inspiring in that regard.

Hand in hand with the fellowship, another key objective was to create a community that revolved around the program. In doing so, we could draw on that network's expertise and also deliver relevant content that could encourage the participation of many more stakeholders. It began small, starting simply with personal contacts from the team, and has grown steadily over the years.

66.
Mycelium architecture sculpture built by the 2021 Fellows under the artistic direction of Maurizio Montalti

Speaking of expertise, could you tell us about the role that mentors play in the fellowship program, and also how they're selected?

The mentors provide inspiration and critical guidance to the fellows. Mentors come from a variety of disciplines and specialties, and are generally invited to share examples from their own, exceptional practices, connected to the topic of each year – such as, for instance, David Zilber, a chef and food scientist who formerly led Noma's fermentation lab. He spoke in 2022 about the notion of metabolism as part of a practice that spans from applications in food to scientific research to material production and so on. We're interested in bringing in sometimes unexpected lecturers who can speak not only to the theoretical, but also provide tangible examples of implementation of those theories reflected in everyday activities.

The beginnings of things are always quite interesting. It's an especially intriguing endeavor to create a program that, if successful, will continue to evolve and extend past your own initial contribution. How did you approach bringing the Academy's overall vision to life, while also laying the groundwork for other thematics and collaborators to follow?

Yes, in this regard, it was essential to create an environment rooted in mutual respect, a space where every voice was given equal weight and where critical and constructive dialogue could flourish. Our learning-by-doing approach aimed to allow each artistic director to identify a relevant subject, which could be analyzed from multiple perspectives by talented fellows, practitioners, and speakers from a variety of disciplines. As artistic director, it was also important to create open frameworks and encourage our participants to help shape those frameworks over the course of our two-week, hyperintense program. In this way, fellows were given responsibility for the program as well, and we were all learning together.

67.
For the dieDAS Fellowship Program 2022, Maurizio Montalti leads a workshop on Collaborating with Fungi: Metabolic Processes for Regenerative Materials and Products

68.
Materials from Montalti's Theater of Experience workshop 2021

The strategy that emerged was to focus on the creative practices as catalysts for analyzing the issues of our day. We used creative and critical thinking and all the tools associated with these practices to consider environmental and social justice issues – all rooted in our relationship to materiality and the site's ecosystem. We believed this was a path that could evolve nicely over time.

I do wish we'd had more means to record our work from the get-go; that was an objective from early on where we fell short. I think it's important to document our pedagogical and collaborative efforts, particularly relating to resonant topics of our era – both for past and future participants as well as the global community. I'm grateful this publication may help communicate some of these efforts, and hope future programs will be similarly well documented.

Given your own professional focus on innovative biomaterials, regenerative design, and the symbiotic relationships between human and nonhuman entities, it's also striking that your approach to the dieDAS program centers a mutually reliant and respectful environment. The horizontal structure of the program reinforces this, as do your chosen thematics. Throughout, you're encouraging a mindfulness about our interconnectivity. It's a really beautiful web you've woven together. Can you speak a bit about this approach?

You phrased it perfectly. Throughout, my wish was to create a program rooted not only in theory, but also in practice and action. In the debut fellowship year, our theme, Farming Materials' Ecologies: From Uncomfortable Pasts to Responsible Futures, we were working with a very bare-bones environment – none of the site renovations had begun or even been formally envisioned at that point. So we saw it as an opportunity to start seeding the ground, not only metaphorically, but also practically, in order to begin reflecting on how fundamental it is to foster a renewed ecosystem on a location that is rooted in a dark past – to show how it is possible to move on to responsible futures, starting from the roots; literally from the soil. So we began planting an ecosystem of different organisms that could support each other – in direct contrast to the repressive spirit of National Socialism that preceded us. We saw an opportunity to work collaboratively as designers, architects, academics and more to lay the foundation for a fully integrated ecosystem in which each actor works in synergy with the others. And this approach continued to evolve and grow over the next two seasons, with Symbiotic Habitat: Growing Regenerative Connections in 2021 and Designing Metabolic Relations – How Can We Build Regenerative Systems? in 2022.

While each program had different nuances and a range of collaborators, cumulatively they were attempts to bring in different perspectives to study ways to reframe our broken relationship to our environment. And to do so, not just theoretically, but also in an immersive, hands-on way.

I believe this laid a strong foundation for all those to follow, and it's been inspiring to watch Germane Barnes's program engage with the site and further shape the dieDAS program. I look forward to all those to come.

Eugenia Morpurgo

dieDAS Head Mentor
(2021–22)

Venice-based designer Eugenia Morpurgo collaborated with dieDAS on the institution's first three fellowship programs. After impressing Artistic Director Maurizio Montalti in her role as a one-day workshop mentor in 2020, he invited her to become head mentor so she could work with him more closely on curriculum development and implementation in 2021 and 2022.

Morpurgo studied social design at the Design Academy Eindhoven (MA, 2011) and industrial design at the Università Iuav di Venezia (BA, 2009). Her research-based practice investigates the potential of agroecology to create regenerative production processes for natural materials, dyes, and binding agents, informed by ecosystem biodiversity and seasonality. Her work has been exhibited at the MAXXI – National Museum of 21st Century Arts in Rome, Triennale Museum in Milan, Total Museum of Contemporary Art in Seoul, Textile Arts Center in New York City, and Z33 House for Contemporary Art, Design & Architecture in Hasselt, among others. Together with Olivia de Gouveia, she founded The Future Continuous.

When did you join the dieDAS team, and what was the length of your tenure?

I started collaborating with dieDAS during the first fellowship in 2020. Artistic Director Maurizio Montalti initially asked me to be a mentor for a one-day workshop. Afterward, he asked me to join in a larger capacity, collaborating with him on the curation of the following two fellowships in 2021 and 2022.

How would you define the overarching vision for dieDAS, and what made you want to be a part of it?

In my view, the vision for dieDAS exists on multiple levels simultaneously. The institution has the goal of becoming a center for contemporary critical culture for the creative industry, rooted in an awareness of the history of the place and the political role that culture can play. Layered on that is the vision that each artistic director brings to the annual fellowship programs, which brings a narrower focus informed by his or her particular areas of interest and research.

For my collaboration with Maurizio, the vision was concentrated on diving deeply into the ecological sustainability of construction materials used in design, from fashion to architecture, working together with the fellows and a cohort of international experts. This specific topic and the dialogical format of the fellowships is what convinced me to be part of it.

How would you define the key objectives of the dieDAS Fellowship Program, and how do the mentors facilitate these objectives?

One key objective is to push the boundaries of the discipline further. The fellows, together with the artistic director and the head mentor, have the opportunity to listen and dialogue with experts from around the world as well as from the region. The international mentors share the most advanced and critical insights into the field, while the local mentors help the fellows to root their reflections in the ecological and historical context in which the fellowship takes place. The time spent questioning and discussing those inputs makes the experience an opportunity for everyone's growth – the participants and the discipline of design and architecture too.

How would you describe your role as head mentor?

In my collaborations with Maurizio on the curation of the fellowship program, we drew on the complementary and overlapping aspects of our practices, especially our approaches to material research. My personal research focuses on agroecological farming practices for material production, while Maurizio's work focuses on bio fabrication. Bringing our perspectives together allowed us to look more critically at the topic of ecological sustainability in construction materials, inspiring us and the fellows to think more deeply about the future of materials and the socioeconomic systems that produce them. The inputs from the invited mentors as well as the critical discussions that the fellows, Maurizio, and I shared has enriched me, both professionally and personally.

69.
An excursion to Weimar during the 2022 dieDAS Fellowship Program: (front row) Tatjana Sprick, Arne Cornelius Wasmuth, Adrian Pepe, Nico Alexandroff, (back row) Steffie de Gaetano, Giulia Pompilj, Maurizio Montalti, and Eugenia Morpurgo

In the role of head mentor for the first years of the fellowship program, how did the program evolve—thinking about the initial vision and then the adaptations and pivots made in response to realities and learnings?

One important element we learned during the first fellowship that strongly influenced the programming of the second one was the element of time. We realized that it was more important to make space for dialogue and reflection during the two weeks rather than filling every moment of the program with an activity. This time for reflection allowed everyone to digest all the enriching content coming from the lectures and trips.

The results of the second fellowship, though, showed us that – given the fellowship's limited, two-week span – it was way more interesting to push the fellows to collaborate. In 2021, they collaborated on creating a small mycelium architecture, and working together toward a common goal pushed them to question their own practice more. In 2022, when they were asked to produce something individually, the fellows fell back to their usual way of working.

70.
For the Fellowship Program 2022, Maurizio Montalti and Eugenia Morpurgo lead a mycelium workshop with designer Julia Lohmann

Please share a few highlights from the fellowship programs you oversaw.

During the 2021 Fellowship, the process of constructing a small architecture using willow and mycelium was a great experience. Moving from listening to lectures about how to relate to nonhuman creatures to having your hands filled with living mycelium that would become a home for humans – all while working in a collaborative manner – spurred deep conversations, which I believe influenced everyone involved.

During the 2022 Fellowship, spending a day foraging the natural surroundings of the dieDAS campus for food, medicine, materials, and dyes allowed us to reflect on the value we give to the species that provide vital resources. It interrupted the distant relations that traditional production and consumption processes establish between the consumer and the origin of the resources we consume.

How would you define the fellowship program's unique contribution to international design culture?

For the individuals who participate, I think it's a great, enriching experience that will influence their practices – which I hope will influence international design culture in the future.

But I believe that if the fellowship programs to date, including the mentor's contributions and the reflections of the fellows, had been well documented, the processes and findings could have been shared widely and become a significant point of reference for international design culture.

How do you hope the program evolves in the future?

I hope that the program finds its footing in the local community and manages to bridge the existing gap between temporary experiences, like the fellowship, and the need for lasting impact made evident by many of the topics addressed.

Zeno Franchini

dieDAS Head Mentor (2023–24) and Fellow (2021)

Palermo-based social designer Zeno Franchini is the current head mentor of the dieDAS Fellowship Program, invited to the position by Artistic Director Germane Barnes. During their two-year tenure, the fellowship curricula have explored social and environmental justice through the themes of Monumental Affairs (2023) and Material Evidence (2024). In 2021, Franchini participated in the dieDAS Fellowship Program as a fellow.

After earning an MA in Social Design from the Design Academy Eindhoven, Franchini cofounded Marginal Studio with designer Francesca Gattello in 2014. The duo produce prototypes, installations, writings, and films that address climate change, decolonization, and political change, with a focus on marginalized communities, neglected environments, and peripheral territories. The studio's work has been exhibited at the 58th Venice Biennale, Manifesta 12, and the Triennale Museum in Milan, among others.

71.
2021 dieDAS Fellows: Pollyanna Moss, Daniel Tish, Carolina Pacheco, and Zeno Franchini

When did you join the dieDAS team, and what was the length of your tenure?

I was invited to submit an application for the 2021 Fellowship. As a social designer based in Palermo, I was captivated by the attitude of openness and the commitment to research that Maurizio Montalti and Eugenia Morpurgo communicated through the call for fellows. Knowing their previous work, I was curious to experience the residency. It's rare in the design world to encounter sincere interest in research and social engagement.

For me, the fellowship was exceptional, and afterward I continued to follow the program's activities and development. Two years later, I found myself under consideration for the head mentor position for the 2023 Fellowship, under the leadership of Artistic Director Germane Barnes. I felt that I could contribute with both an insider and outsider perspective – both through my experience as a participant in the program and through my own experience with Germane's theme for the year, Monumental Affairs.

How would you define the overarching vision for dieDAS, and what made you want to be a part of it?

The open-handed spirit of the fellowship program allows research to be fertile without a strict tie to its outcome. However, the location grounds the work in the immediate context of the architecture and its difficult heritage.

These polarities help to navigate the multiplicity of inputs that are offered by the program. Even though the contributions of participants are diverse, the questions that float in the space are very clear. Understanding the terrible events of our past leads to envisioning a future in which these mistakes are not repeated.

How would you define the key objectives of the dieDAS Fellowship Program, and how do the mentors facilitate these objectives?
The program allows fellows to find their own path – to tackle societal questions from their own point of view. On the curatorial level, the question changes every year, but there remains an underlying attitude that seeks to understand how we can coexist with and inhabit the planet in a more egalitarian and collective society. Each participant brings their own positionality toward the given topic.

How would you describe your role as head mentor?
As head mentor, I coordinate and select the fellowship program's guests and the activities for the fellows. I am a facilitator of the artistic director's vision that works in dialogue with the guests and fellows. I think of the fellowship as an experience composed of a series of moments that extend well beyond the lectures into the shared experiences of strolling, eating, and conversing. These moments help construct the dynamic of exchange between the fellows and their feeling of the place.

72.
2021 dieDAS Fellows weave willow branches to build a mycelium architecture sculpture

How has your work as head mentor impacted your own practice?
In my experience as head mentor, I expanded my understanding of the topic of race in design, which is part of my daily practice working with migrant communities in Palermo. My work is articulated around collective making and material culture as a means to tell stories and find common ground.
Through my work with Germane and the dieDAS program, I had the chance to contribute content based on my personal and professional experiences while also learning more about the African American experience as well as theoretical and academic perspectives on race more broadly – all

set against the backdrop of the racist legacy of Paul Schultze-Naumburg and the Nazi regime.

How would you define the fellowship program's unique contribution to international design culture?

Often in the European design panorama, the more painful and difficult topics are left aside in favor of an unproblematic positivity – which is definitely easier to face but less relevant. With reflections on topics like racism and social exclusion, we can actually contribute to a cultural discourse that benefits society beyond design and architecture. Even in the short time of a fellowship, we can suggest directions, rather than solutions, toward which we can collectively aim.

Within this oasis for design research that's tied to the landscape and the hyperlocal history, I am working toward a future in which colleagues will see this place as a lens through which to critically understand the world in all its inequalities and conflicts.

My hope is that by standing in this place where an oppressive vision was once articulated – a vision that is not so different from the extremist ideologies of today – designers and architects will be able to see their role in undoing harmful structures by embracing the entanglements between all people and beings.

Basse Stittgen

dieDAS Selection
Committee Member (2022) and Fellow (2020)

Born in Hannover and based in Amsterdam, Basse Stittgen was a fellow in the inaugural dieDAS Fellowship Program in 2020, during the tenure of Artistic Director Maurizio Montalti. Two years later, he was invited to help select the fellows for the 2022 fellowship program.

Situated at the intersection of design, art, and material research, Stittgen's practice aims to uncover ways that objects hold the potential to mediate contemporary complexities. Since his graduation from the Design Academy Eindhoven in 2017, his work has been exhibited at the Victoria & Albert Museum, Stedelijk Museum Amsterdam, National Gallery of Victoria, and the 13th Shanghai Biennale of Architecture. His work can also be found in the permanent collections of the MAK Vienna and Museum de Fundatie, among others.

How would you define the overarching vision for dieDAS and its fellowship program, and what made you want to be a part of it?

I experienced dieDAS as a place that aims to create connections, both uplifting and critical, on a multitude of scales – between people and land, people and history, and the program's participants with each other.

I applied for a range of reasons, but most of them relate to my desire to learn and connect. The Saalecker Werkstätten and the hateful ideology that was partially birthed there carry a heavy weight. The program posed a chance for me to confront myself as an artist and a German and for us collectively – the international fellows, mentors, and other collaborators – to dream up and contribute to a new narrative for this place.

74.
Debut dieDAS Fellows 2020: Talin Hazbar, Svenja Keune, and Basse Stittgen

What was the application process like for you? What are some key points you tried to communicate?

I remember one question in the application process about the politics involved in my work. I would not consider myself a political person nor my work intentionally political. I consider myself social and my work socially engaged. Through this approach, my work engages the political by taking a position and by generating attention for what's hidden and overlooked.

101

How did you expect the fellowship to impact your practice?

As my practice is centered around materiality, I saw the fellowship as a chance to deepen my understanding of the entanglements between matter, place, and time and, through that perspective, gain a more fine-grained understanding of material culture. Inspired by the professionals invited by dieDAS, I also looked forward to experimenting with novel design methods and frameworks to critically investigate new socio-material interactions and find ways to position myself in regards to contemporary urgencies in design.

Please share a few highlights from your experience with the fellowship.

The inaugural fellowship took place during the pandemic, and initially there were many questions about whether it could take place at all. So my first highlight would have to be that we could all come to Saaleck and share this space together. Since the pandemic limited our possibilities to actually produce work, we took the chance to collectively think up possible futures for the Saalecker Werkstätten and reflect on our own practices. The open-ended process that was nurtured by the rich lecture program organized by dieDAS is what stays with me.

75.
Mycelium research during the 2020
Fellowship Program

What impact has your experience with the fellowship had so far?

First and foremost, it's the kinship created with everyone involved. I feel part of a community that keeps on growing.

How did you apply your experience as a fellow to your work on the selection committee later on?

For me, material is a lens for the social. So as I reviewed the applications, I was looking for projects that were able to create those links in meaningful ways. I believe this perspective is necessary when engaging with the locality, history, and future of the Saalecker Werkstätten.

What was your experience like working with the other selection committee members?

As a rather young and inexperienced practitioner, it was a bit of a nail-biting experience to join such an esteemed committee. I noticed very quickly, though, that everyone was giving space to each other to speak. And we had a very stimulating conversation since the quality of applications was outstanding.

How do you hope the fellowship program evolves in the future?
I see dieDAS as a place that can push the international design community to rethink its habits, trajectories, and relationships with material bodies. It's a place where we can concern ourselves with what design ought to do – to heal instead of harm.

Sasson Rafailov

dieDAS Selection Committee Member (2023) and Fellow (2020)

Virginia-based designer, craftsperson, and educator Sasson Rafailov was a fellow in the inaugural dieDAS Fellowship Program in 2020, during the tenure of Artistic Director Maurizio Montalti. Two years later, he was invited to help select the fellows for the 2023 fellowship program.

Sasson graduated with a B. Arch from Cornell University in 2018, where he pursued research in design pedagogy. He went on to teach design studio and a foundational theory course at the University at Buffalo's School of Architecture and Planning, and subsequently enrolled in Harvard University's Master of Design Program, where he graduated in 2021. He is currently pursuing a PhD in the Constructed Environment from the University of Virginia School of Architecture. His dissertation proposes a new approach to craft in the educational training of architects and designers through the lens of posthumanist philosophy. The project borrows concepts from new materialist literature, like agential realism, material intelligence, embodiment, and nonhierarchical ontologies, to envision craft production that allows humans to engage with the material world in more ethical and sustainable ways.

How would you define the overarching vision for dieDAS and its fellowship program, and what made you want to be a part of it?

dieDAS is a site of experimentation. In the broadest sense, I understand dieDAS to be changing the relationships that designers have with their communities, from how they approach their own interpersonal networks to how they understand their place among the organisms and materials that define their lives and practices.

The primary vehicle for this reorientation is the exposure of young artists, designers, and craftspeople to new ways of working that challenge their preconceptions and encourage them to build productive new relationships with other fellows, community members in the region, and nonhuman representatives in the landscape and buildings they inhabit.

I was excited to be part of the inaugural group of fellows, because at the time I was searching for new ways to engage with materials in my practice. I was beginning to develop relationships with stone, wood, and clay that went beyond utility and instrumentality, but I was not sure how to explore these new directions.

The theme of the first year's fellowship, Farming Materials' Ecologies, promised to push my understanding of the role of materiality and put me in touch with other designers who might inform my interests. I felt this mission aligned excellently with where I was in my career at the time, and I am grateful to have spent time in Saaleck with the first group of fellows.

What was the application process like for you?

The application asked for quite a bit more than I was used to for a summer fellowship, and so it forced me to reflect on experiences that I did not credit as much as I should have with shaping my approach to design.

I noticed that despite their different wording and apparent shift in focus, the questions were primarily concerned with my views on community and materiality.

I believed my approach to materiality would be unique in the applicant pool, simply because I had experience working in a wide variety of processes that ranged from the traditional wood carving of furniture to the robotic fabrication of architectural components. But it took time for me to recollect experiences wherein I was shaped by my role within design communities.

Reflecting on those occasions, which were greater in number and duration than I had previously thought, I came to a new appreciation for the role of community in my practice. In the application, I wrote about my experiences working in teams in a variety of positions, from leading the design of a barn for the Dilmun Hill Student Farm at Cornell University to working among an international group of students to design and build a gathering space on a remote island in Norway in just one week. I described how these experiences changed the way I approached design work and encouraged me to seek a culture of collaboration in my studio – even if I was not directly conscious of it at the time.

How did you feel when you were notified of your acceptance? How did you expect the fellowship to impact your practice?

I was rather surprised by the acceptance email, not least because in the time between my application submission and their response, the world had come to a halt in the first few months of the COVID-19 pandemic. I was elated to hear that dieDAS was still attempting to host a fellowship that year and anxiously waited for the very rare opportunity to leave for an international trip that would benefit me creatively and educationally.

Since there was no history of the program to respond to, I did not come into the program with any expectations. But I did hope that the people I met would be engaging, knowledgeable, and have interests and experiences that differed from my own.

Please share a few highlights from your experience with the fellowship.

Many of the activities we had planned involved us meeting (often virtually) with designers, historians, artists, and craftspeople from the region and beyond to learn about their practices and how they situated themselves in their contexts. The most memorable of these meetings, for me, was a workshop we did with a natural pigment maker and plasterer in Weimar. Hearing about how she sourced her pigments, the relationships she had with her materials and practice, and how she thought about colors and space was incredibly inspiring.

We also had significant time allotted to pursue our own design work, often in collaboration with other fellows and the artistic director, Maurizio Montalti. Among my favorite design activities was the creation of a swinging bench, which we made from donated wood from the local winery. All of the fellows worked dutifully to restore the lumber, cut the appropriate joinery, and hang the swing on-site – all in a matter of days!

Finally, even though our scheduled activities differed from day to day, we found consistency and community in the meals we had at the Saalecker Werkstätten – all cooked on-site with a level of love and care that made a very foreign, new place feel like home for me. I do not remember how I felt at each meeting with a new academic or artist, and I unfortunately do not recall the details of each of our excursions outside of the Werkstätten, but I remember feeling a sense of peace and kinship at the dining table, sitting with the other fellows and the dieDAS staff as we discussed our plans and favorite moments of the day.

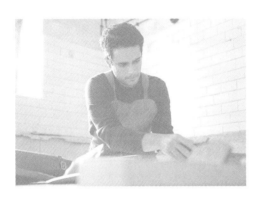

76.
Sasson Rafailov at work during the debut dieDAS Fellowship Program
2020

How has your experience with the fellowship stayed with you? What impact has it had so far?

Given my experience working as a fabrication specialist on several exhibitions, as well as the time I had dedicated to pursuing sculpture and craft, I came to dieDAS with a lot of presuppositions about materials and the processes we have available to work with them. After meeting the other fellows and learning about their work, however, I realized that I had been relying on a rather limited set of material practices to pursue my craft.

What shocked me even more was that their practices began where mine ended. In their studios, several of the fellows, as well as the artistic director, would work with waste – either from other designers or from industries that did not think twice about the byproducts they put out into the world. I was used to saving scraps from my furniture projects, and I knew how to recycle clay, but saving the dust from my sander to feed mycelial cultures, or collecting marble powder from my sculptures to incorporate into clay for handbuilding, represented new and exciting directions for me to pursue in my work when I got home.

I am reminded of the fellowship at dieDAS every time I clean my shop, every time I chip a piece of stone off my latest sculpture, every time I cut into a piece of wood, because my experience inspired me to see creative potential in even the smallest pieces of material, including the dust at my feet.

How did you apply your experience as a fellow to your work on the selection committee later on?

I was honored to be asked to join the selection committee in 2023, and took to evaluating the many applications with great excitement. Based on my experience as a dieDAS Fellow, I knew to look for applicants whose work genuinely matched the theme of the fellowship for sustained periods of time. Anyone could write an application to fit a theme, but genuine commitment to a process or way of working can only be reflected through sustained interest and experimentation over years of dedicated practice and self-education.

I also knew that it would be important to admit fellows whose interests were varied enough that they would be able to learn from and challenge each other – not only because it was important for the artistic director to have a wide variety of skills and talents to pull from for their collaborative work, but also because the fellows learn most from each other. It would be a disservice to that education if they agreed on every aspect of their experience.

Finally, as I was the youngest fellow by a significant margin when I went to Saaleck in 2020, I thought it important to advocate for those young designers who might not have had as much to show in their portfolios or resumes, but who demonstrated passion and promise in the work they had produced until that moment. The mission of dieDAS is dedicated to the future of the design disciplines, and so I believed it needed to bring in fellows of every age to lead their generation towards a more sustainable, collaborative, and ethical future.

What was your experience like working with the other committee members?

The discussions with the other committee members were efficient, thoughtful, and collegial. I had come to expect that kind of experience from dieDAS in general, but I was still happy to see that my voice counted as much as any other member on the committee, and that the other members respected my experience as a fellow and what I brought to the discussion because of it.

We began by reviewing all of the applications independently and by assigning a score to each applicant based on criteria distributed by the dieDAS team. These scores were then added and averaged, and so we began our discussion with the highest scoring applicants and moved down the list over the course of several hours.

I remember our committee reached broad consensus for two of the candidates very quickly because of the high scores we independently assigned them. But the scores for the next few were all about the same, so much of our time was spent listening to each other as we advocated for the applicants who most interested us. Ultimately, I think many of us knew that the applicants we were arguing over would all do well in the fellowship, so we deferred to the preferences of the artistic director, who made his final decision after interviewing several of our top choices.

77.
The 2020 Fellows lunch with dieDAS
patron Egidio Marzona

How do you hope the program evolves in the future?

I look forward to the day when I can walk into the Saalecker Werkstätten to see a big, bustling community of designers congregating around experiments in materiality, technique, and process. Through its expansion, however, I hope the fellowship program maintains the sense of closeness and kinship that I experienced with the three other inaugural fellows in my time there.

The ambitions of the program are grand, and I know the next generation of fellows will appreciate the architectural expansion and renovation of the site, but there is a bond that we first few fellows developed in sleeping in those old buildings, squeezing in around a small dining table, and sharing in the struggle to define the early stages of a program that I hope will not be lost to the future inhabitants of the Werkstätten.

As I've said before, I believe the mission of dieDAS is to create a new design community: one built on trust and collaboration between fellows and their environment; one aimed towards the betterment of society through innovations in design, art, and craft; and one where creative, productive relationships endure long after the fellows return home.

I know the dieDAS team will work hard to meet those first two aims, but the final one is more dependent on the character of the fellows and the experiences they have on-site. It is my hope that future program collaborators will continue to curate a program that allows for this sense of collegiality among fellows for years to come.

Timeline

2020 Farming Materials' Ecologies

ARTISTIC DIRECTOR
Maurizio Montalti

MENTORS
Omer Arbel, Alfredo Brillembourg, Prof. Wulf Diepenbrock, Formafantasma, Alex Marashian, Eugenia Morpurgo, Prof. Dr.-Ing. Daniela Spiegel

SPEAKERS
Glenn Adamson, Christian Benimana, Adib Dada, Anna Heringer, Prof. Dr. h. c. Ákos Moravánszky, Alice Rawsthorn, Celine Vogt, Prof. Sarah M. Whiting

SELECTION COMMITTEE
Maurizio Montalti, Tatjana Sprick, Arne Cornelius Wasmuth

FELLOWS
Talin Hazbar, Svenja Keune, Sasson Rafailov, Basse Stittgen

2021 Symbiotic Habitat

ARTISTIC DIRECTOR
Maurizio Montalti

HEAD MENTOR
Eugenia Morpurgo

MENTORS
Benedikt Bösel, Prof. Rachel Armstrong, Rebecca Burgess, Dr. Daniel Elias, Dr. Jens Eckner, Dipl.-Ing. Jörg Finkbeiner, Gionata Gatto, Martina Köhler, Vivien Sansour, Silke Seibt, Prof. Dr.-Ing. Daniela Spiegel

SPEAKERS
Wava Carpenter, Beatrice Galilee, Fernando Laposse, Prof. Sébastian Marot, Xu Tiantian

SELECTION COMMITTEE
Glenn Adamson, Wava Carpenter, Adib Dada, Maurizio Montalti, Tatjana Sprick, Veit Wagner, Arne Cornelius Wasmuth

FELLOWS
Caroline Pacheco, Zeno Franchini, Pollyanna Moss, Daniel Tish

2022 Designing Metabolic Relations

ARTISTIC DIRECTOR
Maurizio Montalti

HEAD MENTOR
Eugenia Morpurgo

MENTORS
Prof. Rachel Armstrong, Mariana Martinez, Balvanera, Lili Carr, Prof. Jasper Cepl, Dr. Jens Freitag, Klaas Kuitenbrouwer, Prof. Julia Lohmann, Catherine Pfisterer, Christine Rauch, Prof. Dr.-Ing. Daniela Spiegel, Anne van Leeuwen, Prof. Jan Wurm, David Zilber

SPEAKERS
Lars Johan Almgren, Ronald Rael, Alice Rawsthorn , Marcin Rusak, Henry Michael Stephens, Julia Watson

SELECTION COMMITTEE
Glenn Adamson, Nada Debs, Maria Foerlev, Mateo Kries, Maurizio Montalti, Tatjana Sprick, Basse Stittgen, Arne Cornelius Wasmuth

FELLOWS
Nico Alexandroff, Steffie de Gaetano, Adrian Pepe, Giulia Pompilj

2023 Monumental Affairs

ARTISTIC DIRECTOR
Germane Barnes

HEAD MENTOR
Zeno Franchini

MENTORS
Mo Asumang, Nana Biamah Ofuso, Prof. Dr. Kenny R. Cupers, Studio Labour, Ido Nahari Christine Rauch, Prof. Dr.-Ing. Daniela Spiegel

SPEAKERS
Meriem Chabani, Marie-Louise Høstbo, Dr. Mahret Ifeoma Kupka, Karl Monies, Prof. Bryan Lee, Jr., Ravi Naidoo, Prof. Matthias Quent

SELECTION COMMITTEE
Glenn Adamson, Germane Barnes, Tulga Beyerle, Olivier Chow, Folakunle Oshun, Sasson Rafailov, Tatjana Sprick, Arne Cornelius Wasmuth

FELLOWS
Yassine Ben Abdallah, Adam Maserow, Silvia Susanna, Antoinette Yetunde Oni

IV. Voices from the dieDAS Community

"The biggest lesson I acquired from the Fellowship Program lies in the deep intellectual and emotional understanding shared with the other brilliant fellows through a myriad of diverse conversations. This confirms my awareness that design and architecture transcend the mere creation of physical entities; they are intrinsically intertwined with our identities and aspirations, reflecting not only who we are but also who we aspire to become."

Silvia Susanna
Architect and dieDAS Fellow (2023)

"The most significant lesson I learned during my time with the dieDAS Fellowship Program is that designers have the ability to conceive, develop, and disseminate ideologies within and outside of the creative sector. The relationship between design education, architectural aesthetics, material extraction, and the social engineering of communities are all interlinked and shaped by the ideologies of those in power. Learning from the past – specifically from the work of Paul Schultze-Naumburg and his influence within the National Socialist regime – I feel a greater sense of responsibility to counter his approach and use design, architectural practice, and writing to uplift historically marginalized communities and to amplify voices that have been silenced for so long."

Antoinette Yetunde Oni
Artist, Architectural Designer, and Researcher; dieDAS Fellow (2023)

"Wir sind auf einem sehr guten Weg,
hier einen Ort zu schaffen, der
international frequentiert wird und
der Menschen zusammenbringt,
die sich sonst nicht so einfach
begegnen könnten."

Egidio Marzona
Stifter und Vorstand Marzona Stiftung Neue Saalecker Werkstätten

"The program contributed to both personal and professional development. I would've loved to be there longer and spend more time with everyone."

Talin Hazbar

Multidisciplinary Artist and dieDAS Fellow (2021)

"As designers, historians, and citizens of a global world, none of us can afford to turn away from ugly moments that tarnish our collective history. dieDAS enables us to confront our past while not being shackled by it."

Sarah M. Whiting

Dean and Josep Lluís Sert Professor of Architecture, Harvard University Graduate School of Design, and dieDAS Advisory Council Member

"Since all our workshops and activities were group activities, we had a lot of moments to discuss and test our views and get closer as a group."

Basse Stittgen

Designer and dieDAS Fellow (2020)

"I found almost all the events and lectures really valuable and thought provoking in different ways."

Svenja Keune
Artist-Designer and dieDAS Fellow (2020)

"Creating, securing, and maintaining free spaces to give room to unusual ideas is the essential foundation for culture, art, and design. The burdened history of the Saalecker Wekstätten demands that we constantly remind ourselves of the great value of intellectual freedom. In an extraordinary place, dieDAS offers opportunities for urgent and critical discussions of our present as a basis for designing our futures."

Bettina Erzgräber
Professor of Drawing and Visual Arts at Burg Giebichenstein University of Art and Design, and dieDAS Advisory Council Member

"We need to find new ways to tackle the old systems and to reconfigure our relations to the earth and all its inhabitants. Therefore, I believe we need to design new forms of education. This is the reason why I contribute to dieDAS, which is based in a troubled area and where talented young individuals work in a creative spirit of cooperation for the common good."

Hella Jongerius
Designer and dieDAS Advisory Council Member

"This experience was inspiring on so many levels. I come away with a strong sense of community, grateful for the chance to spend time with talented people at different stages of their practices – fellows, mentors, and experts. It was an important reminder that there are so many ways to approach design – and design and nature in particular. There's never just one way of doing things."

Pollyanna Moss
Artist-Designer and dieDAS Fellow (2021)

"My time at dieDAS reinforced the power of empathy. The program encouraged us to look closer at others' experiences – not just humans, but all species – and to learn to dig beyond what you first see. We need to consider how we can use design to better understand, respond to, and narrate the languages of all that surrounds us."

Caro Pacheco
Designer and dieDAS Fellow (2021)

"The dieDAS Fellowship Program is a unique, once in a lifetime experience; you do not want to miss out!"

Steffie de Gaetano
Architect, Interdisciplinary Researcher, and dieDAS Fellow (2022)

"Das Zusammenkommen hier ist etwas ganz Besonderes. Man spürt, wie intensiv sich die Designer*innen miteinander austauschen, und die Themen sind einfach so gut, dass dieses Miteinander tatsächlich in die Zukunft weist."

Andreas Silbersack
Vorstand Marzona Stiftung Neue Saalecker Werkstätten

"The dieDAS Fellowship provides an unmatched opportunity to engage closely with a curious and thoughtful cohort of fellows from all over the world."

Adam Maserow
Architectural Designer, Researcher, and Educator; dieDAS Fellow (2023)

"The most interesting lesson I learned during our investigations is that metabolism – the flow of chemical reactions and energy that sustain living systems – can be cultural as well as physical. We and all things are constantly layering. It is important to recognize that nothing stays the same and to let go of trying to keep things any one way. Only when we master that will we be able to process traumatic histories."

Nico Alexandroff
Research-Architect and dieDAS Fellow (2022) and Selection Committee Member (2024)

"Saaleck provided the perfect opportunity to explore the Monumental Affairs theme. The fellows' ability to witness and augment physical monuments rife with contentious legacies yielded incredible discussions over the length of the fellowship."

Germane Barnes

Founder of Studio Barnes, Associate Professor and the Director
of The Community Housing and Identity Lab at the University of Miami School of Architecture,
and dieDAS Artistic Director (2023–24)

"The dieDAS Fellowship is unique, unlike anything I have participated in before. It creates an environment and comes up with a generous offer to think and try out. The program also allows for exchange between the fellows and the current best minds and partners in the industry to discuss together the challenges we are currently facing."

Adrian Pepe

Artist-Designer and dieDAS Fellow (2022)

"Taking part in the dieDAS Fellowship Program stokes critical questions around the moral basis of art and design that are being answered on the principles of humanism, historical recognition, and territorial introspection. What made the dieDAS Fellowship such a valuable and engrossing experience was witnessing how the theoretical and instructional tools developed during our time together were utilized to redeem marginalized spaces and narratives."

Ido Nahari

Sociologist, Researcher, and Writer; Assistant Editor for *Arts of the Working Class*; dieDAS Fellowship Mentor (2023)

"Die gegenwartskulturelle Transformation der Saalecker Werkstätten ist eine einzigartige Herausforderung, die wir gemeinsam mit kreativen und innovativen Köpfen aus der ganzen Welt in Angriff genommen haben. Schritt für Schritt verwandelt sich das 'unbequeme Denkmal' in einen grundlegend demokratischen Ort, an dem Neues gedacht und entwickelt wird, ohne die langen, finsteren Schatten der Vergangenheit aus dem Blick zu verlieren."

Arne Cornelius Wasmuth

dieDAS Gründungsdirektor

"The dieDAS Fellowship Program provided fertile ground for contemplating the concept of monuments and how we preserve memories within a particular setting. It was a nurturing experience to absorb insights from fellow participants and immerse myself in a community of practitioners that pushes the boundaries of how spaces are designed and experienced."

Yassine Ben Abdallah
Artist-Designer; dieDAS Fellow (2023)

"Today, it is evermore important to realize that the pivotal role of design and creative practices is to catalyze effective change, at both societal and ecosystemic levels. Conscious of such urgencies, the role of organizations like dieDAS is absolutely key. Functioning as a thoroughly inclusive platform — supporting talented creatives in the investigation of complex contemporary subjects, while also fostering deep critical discussions, positive collisions, and unorthodox manifestations of unique collective learning experiences — dieDAS paves the way for new models, challenging the status quo through the introduction of effective paradigm shifts, as driven by intuition, empathy, creativity, and competence."

Maurizio Montalti
Designer, dieDAS Artistic Director (2020–22),
and dieDAS Advisory Council Member

EPILOGUE

Monumental Affairs_Living with Contested Spaces is the very first volume in the Design Akademie Saaleck's new series of publications, the *dieDASdocs*. It presents the results of the dieDAS Fellowship Program in 2023 and the subsequent dieDAS walk + talk Symposium under the artistic direction of the renowned US-American architect Germane Barnes, by whose charisma, equanimity, and intellectual strength I am deeply impressed. My heartfelt gratitude is thus expressed to him for his courage and curiosity in dealing with the "uncomfortable monument" in Saaleck. With *Monumental Affairs*, Germane provides a rich framework for an examination of monuments, including in the international context, and addresses urgent topics like race, ethnicity, nationalism, architecture, and democracy at a historically contaminated site. He takes a detailed look not only at the mechanisms leading to the construction of monuments and the processes of their canonization, but also facilitates a layered and productive program, developed in cooperation with the participating designers, architects, critics, and activists. The present volume exists thanks to them and their dedicated exchange.

When I stood in front of the closed gates of the Saalecker Werkstätten on December 3, 2015, the view through the bars of the main building, which sits high above the Saale River, filled me with horror and yet fascinated me at the same time. The deserted building ensemble seemed almost asleep and enchanted, and yet I knew that here in Saaleck, in this remote location in southern Saxony-Anhalt, important political and social protagonists – Hitler, Goebbels, Frick, Darré, and many more – had come and gone during the darkest epoch in German history. They had taken up the invitation of Paul Schultze-Naumburg, the owner of the property at the time, to exchange their grim ideas and make their evil plans.

After that first encounter, I was unable to get Saaleck out of my mind. When Stephan Kujas, a friend from my student days, told me two years later that the former Saalecker Werkstätten were up for sale, I seized the opportunity and made an appointment to view the site, initially out of sheer curiosity. During my master's studies in protecting European cultural assets at the Europauniversität Viadrina under Prof. Paul Zalewski, I had been intensely focused on "uncomfortable monuments," conducted research on and written about Obersalzberg, and had made a film about coming to terms with the Bückeberg (near Hamelin), the site of the so-called "Reichserntedankfeste" (Reich Harvest Thanksgiving Festival), as a project thesis. These events, staged for propaganda purposes, were the largest mass events of the Third Reich after the Nuremberg Rally. In the case of the Bückeberg, however, the traces of the past were barely discernible, and, until then, there had been no scholarly examination of the location or its history. Single-family houses had meanwhile been constructed on parts of the once expansive grounds in an attempt to reshape the complex history of the location.

The previous owner of the Saalecker Werkstätten had something similar in mind when he purchased the property in the mid-nineteen-nineties. It was hoped that transforming it into a hotel complex would foreground commercial interests without truly dealing with or even touching on its contaminated history at all. The sales brochure from 2017 emphasized the fact that this property offered "a very interesting combination of agricultural and architectural beauty as well as economic opportunities," noting that the "unique property" was also characterized by a "holistic aesthetic that requires a creative approach, based on its heritage as a cultural landscape." "Particularly the 'natural' terrace directly above the Saale River with a splendid view over the river and the surrounding cultural landscape invite designing special locations." There was no mention of the fact that Hitler, who visited the Saalecker Werkstätten in the early nineteen-thirties at Schultze-Naumburg's invitation, had also enjoyed this view.

During this first tour of the property on May 15, 2017 – which included an exploration of the main and adjoining buildings, with their obscure architecture and numerous winding staircases and corridors, small rooms and halls – I was captivated in particular by the kitchen, in addition to the impressive public spaces. It was in this kitchen that the meals for the Nationalist Socialist elites had also been prepared, as well as the food for the residents of the nursing home that was subsequently accommodated in the Saalecker Werkstätten until 1995 and remains in the collective memory of the village today.

78.
The kitchen in the Saalecker
Werkstätten, May 15, 2017

While walking through the deserted and empty kitchen on the lower level of the 1925 annex, the idea occurred to me that the heart of the Saalecker Werkstätten might in the future play a role in an entirely new, inclusive, and democratic framework. And with this vague basic idea in mind, I knocked at Egidio Marzona's door a short time later.

Egidio Marzona is a friend whom I admire and appreciate for so many reasons. Over the decades, he has assembled one of the most important art collections in the country, facilitated the creation of a unique sculpture garden in the Italian Alps, and given the world a unique archive with the AdA – Archiv der Avantgarden in Dresden. Nearly two million archival documents are being successively accessioned and digitized. Every individual document has passed through Egidio's hands, and he has something to say about every sheet of paper, letter, book, picture, chair, and poster and is able to situate the respective document within the history of art and culture. His knowledge is phenomenal, as is his power of imagination. And so he immediately recognized the possibilities that might be generated by transforming the Saalecker Werkstätten, and decided to become involved in realizing the idea. Without his farsightedness, knowledge, and resources, the project in Saaleck would not have come about. To Egidio I express my sincerest gratitude and great appreciation.

In 2018, the two of us, along with attorney Andreas Silbersack, the third member of the board of directors, established the Marzona Stiftung Neue Saalecker Werkstätten. Andreas, who was born in Halle an der Saale, is also a visionary committed with all his heart to the development of his home region, the Federal State of Saxony-Anhalt. He is involved socially and politically in multifaceted ways, and, like Egidio, is dedicated to the opportunities offered by committing to civil society in Saaleck, located at the southernmost tip of the federal state in a region distinguished not only by the beauty of its landscape, but also by its extremely high concentration of ultra-right-wing voters. This is precisely where we would like to set an example, strengthen democracy, promote dialogue, and design something new in community with others.

79.
Marzona Foundation Board of Directors: Arne Cornelius Wasmuth, Egidio Marzona, and Andreas Silbersack, January 1, 2019

With this aim in view, and the active support of the then Bundestag member Rüdiger Kruse, we were given the crucial assurance that we would receive funding from the federal government as well as start-up financing from the Federal State of Saxony-Anhalt. The minister-president, Reiner Haseloff, the minister of state for culture and head of the chancellery office, Rainer Robra, and the current president of the state parliament, Dr. Gunnar Schellenberger, supported the unique public-private partnership with the

Marzona Stiftung, and, in 2019, facilitated the establishment of dieDAS, whose name was inspired by journalist Niklas Maak, who, after touring the Saalecker Werkstätten with us, proposed calling the new project simply the Design Akademie Saaleck – for short, dieDAS.

And this is where Tatjana Sprick, who has contributed decisively to developing the academy's content and structure since the very first phase of its establishment in 2018, comes into play. With her knowledge of the international design world, her broad network, and her passion for people and design, she has made a significant contribution to shaping dieDAS. It is thanks to Tatjana in her role as program and development director that Maurizio Montalti, as the first artistic director, helped conceive and develop the dieDAS Fellowship Program for a period of three years, starting in 2020. Tatjana was subsequently able to engage the enthusiastic interest of Germane Barnes in this position, as well as that of the extremely interesting international designers and architects who support dieDAS in Saaleck as mentors, speakers, and contributors.

80.
The debut dieDAS Fellowship Program 2020: Tatjana Sprick, Arne Cornelius Wasmuth, Maurizio Montalti, Talin Hazbar, Basse Stittgen, Svenja Keune, and Sasson Rafailov

The outstanding transformation of the Saalecker Werkstätten into a site for contemporary culture is the result of a clear vision, hard work, tenacity, and perseverance, but is above all the work of many individuals with a shared goal: reframing the "uncomfortable monument" as a place for innovation and exchange – diverse, interdisciplinary, democratic, and open. I would like to express my thanks to the Danish architect Dorte Mandrup, whose design plan for the restoration in Saaleck has created a suitable framework for the future of dieDAS, as well as to the members of our wonderful advisory council, Omer Arbel, Christian Benimana, Prof. Bettina Erzgräber, Hella Jongerius, Maurizio Montalti, and Prof. Sarah M. Whiting, for their dedication, advice, and good ideas. Gratitude also goes to Johanna Söhningen and Dr. Rainer Schmitz, whose research provides scholarly support for our project, to our staff members Caroline Rebel and Olga Durandina, and to Andra Schumann for her expert assistance in executing the construction plans. Heartfelt thanks are also owed to the engaging authors of this volume; our thoughtful editors, design experts Anna Carnick and Wava Carpenter; and the talented graphic designers Francesca Biagiotti and Francesca Pellicciari of Studio Pupilla; as well as to Lena Kiessler from Hatje Cantz Verlag for the excellent idea of producing *dieDASdocs* as an ongoing series. Thanks, too, to Dorothee Hahn for her skillful project management. I am grateful as well to the patrons of the Marzona Stiftung Neue Saalecker Werkstätten for believing in this project; to the staff of the state chancellery in Magdeburg, Ingo Mundt, Tom Altenburg, and René Richter, for their outstanding commitment; and to Dr. Joachim Scherrieble and Harald Behne from the state administration department for their solution-oriented and pragmatic support. Gratitude is also extended to the funding bodies on the federal and state level, to the Federal Cultural Foundation, which made this volume possible, and to our growing circle of sponsors and partners. The Lord Mayor of the City of Naumburg, Armin Müller, has become a trusted companion and supporter of dieDAS and the Marzona Stiftung, and moreover pampered participants of our walk + talk Symposium on their tour through Naumburg by inviting them to the annual mayor's lunch.

The application documents for the sixth dieDAS Fellowship Program in the summer of 2024 are currently lying on my desk. With his new topic, Material Evidence—The Absence of Land and Labor, Germane Barnes will once again bring together a highly motivated group of innovative and daring designers, architects, and craftspeople in Saaleck. It is these young talents who must be thanked first and foremost for the fact that dieDAS is developing into the location we envisioned, a place where, on the foundation of its weighty past, we are building something constructive and collective and searching for better, innovative approaches to solutions for our shared future. Thank you to all the dieDAS fellows for realizing this vision. And, last but not least, a heartfelt thank you to Andrea Sprick and Oscar Casas Pinto for taking care of us so lovingly during the fellowships in Saaleck, to our facility manager, Ralf König, and to our neighbor Karl-Heinz Tischner, without whose help the lime trees in the garden would run rampant.

The planning and building permit for the rehabilitation of the site has been granted, and the funding stands at the ready. The project will enter its next phase in 2024, and I am deeply humbled and grateful to have the opportunity to be part of it.

Arne Cornelius Wasmuth

81. Saalecker Werkstätten

33. Egidio Marzona reading a book in the Saalecker Werkstätten garden

Deutsche Texte

VORWORT

Die Saalecker Werkstätten sind ein „unbequemes Denkmal". Als wir das imposant über der Saale thronende Ensemble mit seinem dunklen Schatten 2017 das erste Mal gemeinsam erlebt haben, wurde schnell der Plan geschmiedet, diesen historisch belasteten Ort gegenwartskulturell zu transformieren. Das war die Geburtsstunde der dieDAS – Design Akademie Saaleck.

Heute wütet in Europa Krieg, rechtsextreme Parteien erstarken, die Energiepreise steigen in schwindelerregende Höhen und unsere Umwelt ächzt unter den Auswirkungen globaler Klimakrisen. Im Kontext dieser immensen Herausforderungen hinterfragen wir die Ursachen und suchen gleichzeitig nach innovativen Lösungsansätzen. Dabei ist eine kritische Auseinandersetzung mit unserer Vergangenheit ebenso erforderlich wie die Förderung zukunftsweisender Alternativen. Genau an dieser Schnittstelle engagiert sich dieDAS. Die Akademie wurde gegründet, um Gestalter*innen und Kreativen Entwicklungs- und Vernetzungsmöglichkeiten zu bieten – und dies aus der tiefen Überzeugung heraus, dass diese „Ressourcen" und offenen Räume wesentlich sind für ein gelöstes Arbeiten an innovativen und gesellschaftlich relevanten Prozessen, die unsere Gegenwart und unser künftiges Miteinander bereichern.

2018 erwarb der Sammler und Mäzen Egidio Marzona die ehemaligen Saalecker Werkstätten und ermöglichte so die Entstehung der Marzona Stiftung Neue Saalecker Werkstätten. Das Objekt blickt zurück auf eine bewegte und schwerwiegende Vergangenheit, die unweigerlich an die Person des Architekten und späteren Rassenideologen Paul Schultze-Naumburg geknüpft ist: 1902 baute dieser in Saaleck sein Wohnhaus und gründete kurz darauf die Saalecker Werkstätten, die sich auch zu einem Plateau für nationalsozialistisches Gedankengut entwickelten. An diese Geschichte muss erinnert werden. Das kollektive Gedächtnis darf niemals vergessen, was in den Saalecker Werkstätten einmal ausgesprochen wurde.

Genau dieses „unbequeme Denkmal" jetzt als neuen Ort des freien Denkens, des Gestaltens und des Diskurses aufzubauen, ist für die Marzona Stiftung eine bewusst getroffene Wahl. Die ehemaligen Saalecker Werkstätten werden durch dieDAS einem produktiven Austausch gewidmet und einer internationalen Gemeinschaft zur Verfügung gestellt. Zwischen Stipendiat*innen, Wissenschaftler*innen, Partnerinstitutionen und einem weltweiten Netzwerk von Designer*innen, Architekt*innen, Handwerker*innen und Künstler*innen entsteht in Saaleck ein Ort für weite Gedanken und Visionen – divers, interdisziplinär, offen. Im Fokus stehen Themen wie Materialökologie, Nachhaltigkeit und Bio-Design ebenso wie Klima, Gerechtigkeit und Demokratie.

Seit 2020 finden auf dem Gelände der neuen Saalecker Werkstätten erste Veranstaltungen statt. Am Tag der offenen Tür laden wir regelmäßig Interessierte aus Saaleck und der Umgebung ein, um den Ort zu erkunden und seine Entwicklung persönlich mitzuerleben. Gemeinsam mit einem Team hoch engagierter Mitarbeiter*innen und wechselnden Künstlerischen Leitungen haben wir mit dem jährlichen dieDAS Fellowship-Programm und dem dieDAS walk + talk Symposium zwei Formate entwickelt, die Saaleck schon heute weit über die Landesgrenzen hinaus als Ort des freien Denkens und der Kreativität etablieren.

Mit dem Architekten Germane Barnes erlebt dieDAS einen Künstlerischen Leiter, der sich dem Denkmal aus gesellschaftspolitischer Perspektive annähert und dazu auffordert, die Architektur als Vehikel für eine alternative Geschichtsschreibung zu verstehen. *Monumental Affairs: Leben mit umstrittenen Orten* stellt sich der kontaminierten Vergangenheit des Ortes sowie seinem umstrittenen Erbe und untersucht die Narrative, Notwendigkeit und Kanonisierung von Gebäuden und Monumenten. Barnes fragt: Wer bestimmt, welche Architektur in diesen Kanon eingeht? Welche offensichtlichen und auch subtilen Formen der Unterdrückung sind dabei am Werk? Und wie lässt sich der Begriff des öffentlichen Raumes dazu verwenden, einmal kanonisierte Denkmale zu demontieren? Ziel ist es somit auch in dieser Publikation, gegenwärtige Formen von Rassismus und Diskriminierung in der gebauten Umwelt kritisch zu reflektieren.

dieDAS – Design Akademie Saaleck fördert Veränderung und die Wandlung der historisch kontaminierten Anlage zu einem kulturellen Leuchtturm, dessen Licht weit über die Grenzen Saalecks und Naumburgs hinaus sichtbar werden möge. Wir stehen am Anfang eines mehrjährigen Sanierungsvorhabens nach dem Masterplan der dänischen Architektin Dorte Mandrup. Die Gebäude werden in den kommenden Jahren sukzessive ihrer neuen Nutzung zugeführt, sodass neben der Design Akademie auch zunehmend Veranstaltungen, Workshops und thematisch relevante Angebote für Interessierte aus der näheren Umgebung stattfinden können. Auf diesem Weg werden wir ent-

133

scheidend durch das Land Sachsen-Anhalt und die Bundesrepublik Deutschland unterstützt und von engagierten Partnern aus dem In- und Ausland begleitet.

Inmitten von Deutschland wird mit der Design Akademie Saaleck in Europa und der Welt ein entschlossenes und erfahrbares Zeichen gesetzt für uneingeschränkte Gestaltungsfreiheit und die Veränderungskraft einer demokratischen Gesellschaft.

Egidio Marzona, Andreas Silbersack und Arne Cornelius Wasmuth Vorstand der Marzona Stiftung Neue Saalecker Werkstätten

EINLEITUNG

Monumental Affairs: Leben mit umstrittenen Orten stellt eine grundsätzliche Frage: Was ist ein Denkmal? Traditionell sind mit diesem Begriff physische Monumente gemeint, die mit der ausdrücklichen Absicht errichtet wurden, an Personen, Orte oder Ereignisse zu erinnern, welche ihre jeweiligen Gesellschaften geprägt haben. Üblicherweise werden solche Monumente oder Denkmäler als dauerhafte, unveränderliche und hochgradig sichtbare Zeugnisse für gegenwärtige und zukünftige Generationen gebaut, um bestimmte Taten, Momente und Werte zu würdigen, die niemals in Vergessenheit geraten sollen.

Die Entscheidung, wer oder was es würdig ist, mit einem Denkmal geehrt zu werden – und damit auch zu bewerten, welche gemeinschaftlichen Tugenden gefeiert und bewahrt werden sollen –, ist in der Geschichte meist jenen vorbehalten gewesen, die die größte wirtschaftliche, gesellschaftliche und politische Macht besaßen. Folglich dienen die sichtbarsten und beeindruckendsten Monumente – sowie die Werte, die sie verkörpern – oft dazu, bestehende Hierarchien zu stärken und ungerechte Systeme zu bestätigen, die darauf abzielen, marginalisierte und abweichende Stimmen zu unterdrücken. Heute, inmitten wachsender Kritik an den anhaltenden Auswirkungen tief verwurzelter Ungleichheit, Ausbeutung und Unterdrückung, beginnt die traditionelle Definition dessen, was ein Denkmal ausmacht, und wer darüber entscheidet, zu bröckeln.

Vor diesem kritischen Hintergrund geht die vorliegende Publikation – das erste Buch der dieDAS – Design Akademie Saaleck – von einer expansiven und progressiven Interpretation des Denkmals aus und untersucht damit auch eine weitere komplexe Fragestellung: Wenn Denkmale als Verkörperungen des kollektiven Gedächtnisses einer Gesellschaft, ihrer gemeinsamen Ideale und einheitsstiftenden Identität verstanden werden, wie können sie dann so konzipiert, konstruiert und konserviert werden, dass sie eine größere Vielfalt an Perspektiven repräsentieren, unterdrückende Machtstrukturen auflösen und positiven Wandel in einer Welt fördern, die von zunehmenden Krisen sowohl der Gesellschaft als auch der Umwelt geprägt ist?

Der Titel und das Thema von *Monumental Affairs_Living with Contested Spaces* wurde durch den Künstlerischen Leiter der dieDAS – Design Akademie Saaleck, Germane Barnes, für das dieDAS Fellowship-Programm 2023 und das dieDAS walk + talk Symposium konzipiert. Mit dem diskursiven

Rahmen, den er in seinem Kuratoren-Statement definiert und in seinem Programm an der dieDAS weiterentwickelt hat, lud der in Miami lebende Architekt und Dozent die Teilnehmer und Teilnehmerinnen dazu ein, Denkmale und die Errichtung von Denkmalen über die konventionellen Definitionen hinaus zu untersuchen, dabei die Heterogenität von – formalen und informellen, absichtlichen und unabsichtlichen, positiv konnotierten und problembehafteten – Denkmalen anerkennend, auch in Bezug auf Themen wie Rassismus, Migration, Vertreibung und Nationalismus.

Barnes' Kernthese basiert auf einer ihr zugrunde liegenden Annahme: Die Strukturen, die wir errichten, sind untrennbar mit den Werten verflochten, die wir vertreten. In dieser Hinsicht rückt der veränderliche und subjektive Charakter eines Denkmals in den Fokus. Im Laufe der Entwicklung einer Gesellschaft werden die Monumente ihrer Vergangenheit zwangsläufig immer wieder neu bewertet und mitunter sogar angefochten. Forderungen, neue Denkmale zu errichten und alte zu vernichten, kommen auf und geraten in Konflikt miteinander. Hinzu kommt, dass auch existierende Bauten einen Status als Denkmal erlangen können – zum Beispiel aus historischen, handwerklichen oder baukünstlerischen Gründen –, selbst wenn sie ursprünglich gar nicht als solche konzipiert worden sind. Wenn wir den Rückkopplungseffekt zwischen dem, was wir kollektiv wertschätzen, und dem, was wir kollektiv bauen, genauer untersuchen, so erweitern wir unser Verständnis von Denkmälern. Wir beginnen zu begreifen, dass diese überall um uns herum existieren, wo immer gesellschaftliche Gruppen die Wirkung von kulturellen, wirtschaftlichen und politischen Ideologien erleben, die sich in ihrer physischen Umgebung manifestieren. Unsere Städte, Landschaften und Häuser sind allesamt auf ihre jeweilige Art Denkmäler für die Systeme, in denen sie entstanden sind.

Im ersten Abschnitt dieses Buches unter dem Titel „Monumental Affairs" steht Barnes' multidimensionale Hypothese im Mittelpunkt und hinterfragt unser Verständnis von Denkmälern anhand von fünf unterschiedlichen und doch komplementären, zum Nachdenken anregenden Essays. Vier der fünf Autoren und Autorinnen dieses Abschnitts haben beim dieDAS walk + talk Symposium 2023 Vorträge gehalten – unter ihnen Barnes selbst.

In seinem Essay „Die Macht der Architektur" beleuchtet Barnes, wie seine persönlichen Erfahrungen ihm auf vielfältige Art und Weise verdeutlicht haben, dass Architektur sowohl theoretisch als auch praktisch Machtstrukturen aufrechterhalten und ihnen gleichzeitig entgegenwirken kann. Dieser Fokus hat wiederum seine Sicht auf die Programmgestaltung für dieDAS beeinflusst.

In „Gedächtnis ist Impuls" teilt der in New Orleans lebende Architekt und Design-Justice-Aktivist Bryan C. Lee Jr. eine ergreifende persönliche Geschichte. Er schildert die unsäglichen Erlebnisse seines Urgroßvaters, der als Schwarzer ein Haus in einer weißen Nachbarschaft kaufen wollte. Diese Geschichte verdeutlicht eine weiße Vormachtstellung, die zutiefst in der existierenden Vorherrschaftsideologie der US-amerikanischen Gesellschaft verankert ist. Lee tritt dafür ein, Design als Werkzeug des Protests und als Waffe gegen etablierte Systeme einzusetzen, die Schwarzen und Braunen Communities Wohlstand, Gesundheit und Chancengleichheit vorenthalten.

Die in Paris ansässige Architektin und Stadtplanerin Meriem Chabani argumentiert in ihrem Essay „Heiligtümer der Fürsorge in unsicheren Zeiten", dass unsere gegenwärtigen globalen Krisen – vom Klimawandel bis hin zu um sich greifenden gesellschaftlichen Unruhen – das unausweichliche Resultat einer kapitalistischen Hegemonie sind. Von einem korrupten Ethos befeuert, wird alles und jede/r auf der Erde als Ware und Futtermittel im Streben nach grenzenlosem Wirtschaftswachstum betrachtet. Der Weg zu einer gerechteren und widerstandsfähigeren Welt beginnt Chabani zufolge damit, eine Kultur der Fürsorge für den Planeten und alle seine Bewohnerinnen und Bewohner zu kultivieren und zu pflegen, was bedeutet, ausgewählte Ressourcen als heilig, unverletzlich und im Kontext flüchtigen Gewinnstrebens für tabu zu erklären. In ähnlicher Weise enthüllt der Rechtsextremismusforscher und Professor für Soziologie, Matthias Quent, die schädlichen Auswirkungen unmenschlicher und auf Unterdrückung basierender Weltanschauungen, insbesondere reaktionärer, rechter soziopolitischer Strömungen unter dem Deckmantel des Naturschutzes. In seinem Essay „Räume und Ideologien der Ungleichheit in der Klimakrise" warnt er vor den heimtückischen pseudowissenschaftlichen Lügen, die den Sozialdarwinismus des Fressen-und-gefressen-Werdens sowie einen xenophoben Ökofaschismus untermauern und für unzählige Gewalttaten gegen Mensch und Umwelt verantwortlich sind.

Die in Cambridge (Massachusetts) lebende Architektin und Wissenschaftlerin Sarah M. Whiting, Dean der Harvard Graduate School of Design (GSD) und Mitglied des dieDAS Kuratoriums, schließt den ersten Abschnitt der vorliegenden Publikation ab. In ihrem Artikel „Beständigkeit und Komplexität von Denkmalen" hinterfragt Whiting die Entwicklung von Denkmalen während der vergangenen hundert Jahre und präsentiert einige vielversprechende Entwicklungen in Praxis und Theorie des 21. Jahrhunderts, darunter auch Arbeiten, die an der Harvard GSD und an der dieDAS entstanden sind. Auch Whiting betont, dass Architektur und Design nicht nur unsere gebaute Umgebung prägen, sondern auch die Werte, die sie vermitteln.

Barnes' Thema *Monumental Affairs* greift über das Jahresprogramm 2023 hinaus die grundsätzlichen Ziele der dieDAS auf und wirft ein Licht auf die vor fünf Jahren von der Marzona Stiftung Neue Saalecker Werkstätten konzipierten Visionen. Einerseits ist dieDAS eine Akademie, die sich der Zusammenführung von interdisziplinären, intersektional praktizierenden und divers denkenden Menschen widmet, die an aktuellen Themen in Design, Architektur und Handwerk arbeiten. Hier sollen innovative, sozialverantwortliche Ansätze zu global relevanten Fragen in einer Atmosphäre des offenen Austauschs erkundet werden. Andererseits setzt sich dieDAS aber auch mit der dunklen Geschichte des Orts auseinander, an dem sie beheimatet ist. Die Saalecker Werkstätten wurden von dem Rassenideologen Paul Schultze-Naumburg kurz nach der Wende zum 20. Jahrhundert gegründet und gelten heute als „unbequemes Denkmal". Die vorliegende Publikation reflektiert daher in einer Reihe von Essays und Interviews die Vision der dieDAS, eine Brücke der Aussöhnung zwischen einem historischen Versagen und einer besseren Zukunft zu schlagen, indem sie das Potenzial von Bildung, Dialog und kreativer Kollaboration zu nutzen versucht.

Der Abschnitt II, „Saalecker Werkstätten", beschäftigt sich mit dem Ziel der dieDAS, die Anlage in Saaleck gegenwartskulturell zu transformieren. In ihrem Essay „Die Saalecker Werkstätten als unbequemes Erbe" zeichnet Daniela Spiegel, Professorin für Denkmalpflege und Baugeschichte an der Fakultät Architektur und Urbanistik der Bauhaus-Universität Weimar, die hasserfüllte Geschichte der Saalecker Werkstätten nach. Darüber hinaus erörtert sie, warum der dunkle Schatten, den ihr Erbauer Paul Schultze-Naumburg hinterlassen hat, weder aus dem kollektiven Gedächtnis gelöscht noch in eine traditionelle Denkmalwürdigung erhoben werden sollte. Als unbequemes Denkmal müssen die Saalecker Werkstätten so transformiert werden, dass das Ergebnis der Gesellschaft zugutekommt,

und zwar in direktem Widerspruch zu den hier einst postulierten rassistischen und antisemitischen Ideen. In „Die Saalecker Werkstätten. Transformation eines unbequemen Denkmals" skizziert Stephan Kujas, Kulturwissenschaftler und Denkmalpfleger der Stadt Weißenfels, wie dieDAS dieses Ziel zu erreichen versucht. Einerseits soll ein Dokumentationszentrum und Lernort entstehen, der das Wissen um die Vergangenheit des Ortes aufarbeitet und vermittelt; andererseits stellt sich die Akademie in den Dienst der Förderung kollaborativer und demokratischer gesellschaftlicher Prozesse, weit über den regionalen Raum hinaus.

Der Essay der in Kopenhagen lebenden Architektin Dorte Mandrup mit dem Titel „Die Saalecker Werkstätten – ausstellen, lassen, hinzufügen" blickt voraus auf das bevorstehende transformative Kapitel der Saalecker Werkstätten. Mandrups Masterplan für die Restaurierung der Anlage, der in den kommenden Jahren fertiggestellt wird, ermöglicht es der dieDAS, ein größeres Publikum in Saaleck willkommen zu heißen und ihre Mission umzusetzen.

Abschnitt III trägt den Titel „dieDAS – Design Akademie Saaleck" und gibt einen Überblick über die Entwicklungsgeschichte der dieDAS während der wegweisenden ersten fünf Jahre. Diese werden durch eine Reihe von Interviews mit prägenden Teammitgliedern und Teilnehmer*innen der dieDAS Programme vermittelt. Insgesamt bilden diese persönlichen Berichte eine umfassende Oral History der Konzeptualisierung und Umsetzung der zentralen dieDAS Initiativen ab, wie das jährliche Fellowship-Programm, das dieDAS walk + talk Symposium und vieles andere mehr. Die Stimmen, die hier zu Wort kommen, belegen das kollaborative Potenzial der dieDAS Programme und zeichnen ein eindrucksvolles Bild der Ergebnisse, die bereits in der Design-Community in der Region im südlichen Sachsen-Anhalt und weit darüber hinaus spürbar sind.

Jedes Jahr versammelt sich eine neue Gruppe von internationalen Fellows, Mentor*innen, Referent*innen und Besucher*innen an der dieDAS, um das unbequeme Denkmal zu hinterfragen und zu transformieren. Dabei nutzen sie die unerschöpfliche kreative Werkzeugkiste des Designs, um Themen von globaler Relevanz zu analysieren und neu zu denken. Statt die Saalecker Werkstätten zu einem Museum zu machen oder ihre dunkle Vergangenheit zu verschleiern, ist dieDAS entschlossen, ein Denkmal des Schmerzes in ein Symbol der Hoffnung zu verwandeln und so einen sich entwickelnden Raum des Lernens, des Diskurses und der präzisen Auseinandersetzung

136

mit der Geschichte zu ermöglichen. Es entsteht ein dynamisches Designlabor, in dem vorausschauende und leidenschaftliche Talente aus der ganzen Welt durch eine Vielfalt an Perspektiven, Erfahrungen und Expertisen miteinander kooperieren, um eine gerechtere, bessere und nachhaltigere Zukunft zu gestalten. Innerhalb dieses besonderen Mikrokosmos, am Knotenpunkt seines kreativen und kulturellen Austauschs, arbeiten dieDAS und eine wachsende Community von Partner*innen daran, gemeinsam eine Welt zu erschaffen, in der wir in Zukunft miteinander leben wollen.

Anna Carnick und Wava Carpenter
Kuratorinnen, Redakteurinnen und
Gründerinnen von Anava Projects

I. MONUMENTAL AFFAIRS: LEBEN MIT UMSTRITTENEN ORTEN

Statement zum dieDAS Fellowship-Programm 2023

Da traditionell vom Diskurs ausgeschlossene Stimmen zunehmend das Versagen und die diskriminierenden Praktiken von Architektur und Stadtplanung aufdecken, wird eine konstruktive, holistische Untersuchung dieser Disziplinen immer dringlicher. Globaler Terror und Dissens, die typischerweise als politisch und militaristisch charakterisiert werden, offenbaren allmählich ihre räumlichen Einflüsse. Designgerechtigkeit zwängt sich durch Ritzen, die bei herkömmlicher Architekturtheorie und -diskurs meist verschlossen bleiben. Diese Verschiebung hin zu einem eher egalitären und nichtwestlichen intellektuellen Ansatz ist der Antrieb für das dieDAS Fellowship 2023: *Monumental Affairs*. In diesem Zusammenhang stehen Designer*innen, Theoretiker*innen, Architekt*innen, Kritiker*innen und Menschen aus anderen Disziplinen vor der Herausforderung, die Notwendigkeit von Denkmalen zu hinterfragen.

Monumental Affairs stellt die Frage: Wie kommt der Prozess der Kanonisierung zum Tragen? Wer bestimmt, welche Architektur von welchem Zeitpunkt an zum Kanon gehört? Welche offenen oder subtilen Formen der Unterdrückung sind in diesem Prozess angelegt? Wie nutzt man den öffentlichen Raum, um diese kanonisierten Denkmäler beziehungsweise Denkmale zu demontieren?

Im burgenländischen Saaleck, im ehemaligen Wohnhaus des Architekten und rassistischen Vordenkers Paul Schultze-Naumburg (einst ein Treffpunkt für Nationalsozialisten), bietet dieDAS ihren Fellows eine zwar belastete, aber gleichwohl fruchtbare Umgebung, um taktischen Urbanismus als Mittel des architektonischen und räumlichen Widerstands einzusetzen. Für die Dauer ihres Aufenthalts wird die interdisziplinäre Gruppe den Versuch unternehmen, Architektur als Vehikel alternativer Geschichte(n) zu nutzen. Die Spekulationen über Designideen werden durch Workshops zu Themen wie Rassismus, Ethnie, Migration, Vertreibung und Nationalismus unterstützt. *Monumental Affairs* weiß um die ehemals nationalistische Agenda dieses historischen Standorts, sein umstrittenes Erbe und seine damals explizite Ausgrenzung nicht-weißer Baumeisterinnen und Baumeister.

Indem diese Themen ganz direkt angesprochen werden – und unter Berücksichtigung der Dringlichkeit, die unser aktuelles globales Klima gebietet, schafft dieDAS einen Ort der Schaffenskraft, der Reflexion und der Ideen.

Germane Barnes
Künstlerischer Leiter dieDAS 2023

138

DIE MACHT DER ARCHITEKTUR

Germane Barnes

Architekt, Gründer des Studio Barnes, Associate
Professor und Director of The Community Housing
and Identity Lab an der University of Miami, School
of Architecture sowie Künstlerischer Leiter dieDAS
(2023–2024)

Mein Leben hat sich am 9. September 2004 von Grund auf verändert. An jenem Tag bekam ich einen Anruf von meinem Vater mit der Nachricht, dass meine ältere Schwester ihren Kampf gegen den Krebs verloren hatte. Es war mein erstes Jahr im College, wo ich Architektur an der University of Illinois Urbana-Champaign studierte. Der Anruf erreichte mich am frühen Morgen. Ich erinnere mich an dieses Detail, weil ich mich nach dem Gespräch wie unter Schock anzog und in den Kurs „Design Studio 1" ging, der wie immer um neun Uhr anfing.

Ich wollte schon immer Architekt werden. Nachdem ich jedoch meine Schwester verloren hatte, zerbrach meine Beziehung zur Architektur. Ich war immer ein willensstarker, selbstmotivierter Student gewesen. Jetzt tat ich mich schwer, mich auf mein Studium zu konzentrieren. Ich fand nicht zurück zu der Begeisterung und der Beharrlichkeit, die mich erfüllt hatten, ehe ich auf dem Campus ankam. Je näher ich meinem Abschluss kam, desto mehr wurde mir klar, dass ich so nicht zur Graduate School zugelassen werden würde, da meine Noten und meine Mappe zweifelsohne unterdurchschnittlich waren. Also entschloss ich mich, meine Ambitionen auf ein Graduiertenstudium zurückzustellen und mir erst einmal eine Anstellung zu suchen. So kam ich zu meinem ersten Praktikum in Kapstadt. Es handelte sich um ein Architekturbüro, das auf hochwertige Wohnprojekte spezialisiert war und pro bono in Armenvierteln arbeitete. Und das war für mich der Wendepunkt.

Es war in dem Township Khayelitsha, wo ich mich inmitten zwangsumgesiedelter, unterversorgter Communities Architektur widmete, dass ich erstmals mit sozial engagiertem Design in Berührung kam. Dort erkannte ich die Macht der Architektur: ihre Fähigkeit zu unterjochen und zu unterdrücken – und umgekehrt, aufzurichten. Ich sah mit eigenen Augen die krassen Ungleichheiten im Zugang zu Ressourcen und Möglichkeiten. Das weckte in mir eine Leidenschaft, Design einzusetzen, um systemischen Ungerechtigkeiten entgegenzuwirken und Communities am Rand der Gesellschaft zu ermächtigen.

Schon immer habe ich die gebaute Umgebung genau beobachtet. Als Kind verbrachte ich täglich mehrere Stunden auf dem Weg zur Schule und zurück in einem Bus, der meine Heimatstadt Chicago durchquerte. Ich musste vom entlegenen Rand der West Side, wo ich wohnte, an die North Side und später nach Downtown. Ich beobachtete den Wandel der Stadtlandschaft von Arbeiterwohnungen zu eleganten Einfamilienhäusern und schließlich zu riesigen Hochhäusern, die unerreichbar schienen für Menschen, die so aussahen wie ich. Doch meine Ausbildung in Südafrika stärkte mein Bewusstsein für meine eigene Handlungsmacht. Dieses Erlebnis entfachte den Funken, der seither meine gesamte Herangehensweise an Architektur und Forschung mit Leben erfüllt. Ich werde von dem Imperativ angetrieben, Architektur als Werkzeug für sozialen Wandel einzusetzen. Meine Lebenserfahrung hat ein tiefes Engagement für Gleichheit, Nachhaltigkeit und Menschenwürde in mir verankert. Dies manifestiert sich in einer Praxis, die Kooperation und Community in den Mittelpunkt stellt und Räume entwirft, die ermächtigen, heilen und sozialen Zusammenhalt fördern. Das motiviert mich dazu, inklusive Designpraktiken zu befürworten und den architektonischen Kanon zu erweitern, sodass die Bedürfnisse und die Stimmen jener, die von der westlich orientierten Pädagogik gewohnheitsmäßig ignoriert und übergangen werden, Priorität und Sichtbarkeit erfahren.

Das Feld der Architektur wird seit Langem von weißen Perspektiven dominiert, was zu einem erheblichen Mangel an Schwarzen Architekt*innen führt. Diese Unterrepräsentanz spiegelt nicht nur systemische Ungleichheiten wider, sondern perpetuiert auch einen Teufelskreis der Marginalisierung in der gebauten Umgebung. Als kulturelle Ausdrucksform und als Machtinstrument spielt Architektur eine entscheidende Rolle bei der Gestaltung sozialer, wirtschaftlicher und räumlicher Dynamiken von Communities. Schnellstraßen durchschneiden Stadtbezirke, Enteignungen „rechtfertigen" Zerstörung, und Gentrifizierung heizt den Verdrängungsprozess an. Betonmonstrositäten schaffen zwar öffentliche Infrastruktur, lassen sich angesichts ihrer Monumentalität jedoch auch als Denkmale betrachten: Sie verkörpern und symbolisieren Dominanz und Gewalt. Unter diesen Umständen trägt Architektur aktiv dazu bei, die Stimmen von Minderheiten zum Schweigen zu bringen und auszulöschen, indem sie die bestehenden Machtstrukturen verstärkt und räumliche Rassentrennung fortwährend fördert.

So entstand die Idee zum Programm *Monumental Affairs*. Es ist schlicht unmöglich, den Gebäudekomplex in Saaleck zu besuchen, der von einem rassistischen Ideologen geschaffen wurde, ohne zu erkennen, dass es sich um einen Ort handelt, der eine Form der Unterdrückung darstellt. Paul Schultze-Naumburgs Vermächtnis ist eines des Hasses und materialisiert sich in einem skulptural eingebetteten Frankenstein-Bau. Hier treffen unterschiedliche Ebenen der Geschichte ebenso aufeinander wie aktuelle Gespräche über Arbeit, Migration, Xenophobie und vieles mehr. Es handelt sich zweifellos um ein monumentales Denkmal.

Denkmale sind greifbare Symbole für Geschichte, Kultur und Macht, können jedoch auch als umstrittene Orte existieren, an denen sich Narrative des Kolonialismus und Rassismus überschneiden. Als solche laden sie dann zur Auseinandersetzung ein. Im Laufe der Geschichte wurden Denkmäler errichtet, um an Individuen, Ereignisse oder Ideologien zu erinnern. Sie spiegeln in den meisten Fällen die Werte der dominierenden gesellschaftlichen Gruppen wider. Viele historische Denkmäler ehren und erinnern jedoch an Persönlichkeiten, die an kolonialer Ausbeutung, Sklaverei und anderen Formen der Unterdrückung beteiligt waren. Der hiesige Standort, heute dieDAS, bildet da keine Ausnahme. Hitler persönlich wurde hier einst begeistert begrüßt.

Der Fortbestand solcher Denkmale in der gebauten Umgebung kann ein Vermächtnis der Ungleichheit und Ungerechtigkeit aufrechterhalten und Narrative verfestigen, die die Erfahrungen unterdrückter Communities marginalisieren oder sogar auslöschen. Sie können als Erinnerung an historisches Unrecht und an den fortwährenden Kampf um Gleichheit und Gerechtigkeit dienen. In manchen Fällen bieten sie die Grundlage für einen konstruktiven Diskurs. Im Rahmen des Fellowship-Programms *Monumental Affairs* haben wir Stimmen aus aller Welt eingeladen, sich mit diesem Ort auseinanderzusetzen. Sie brachten ein breites Spektrum an Perspektiven ein und ermöglichten so tiefgehende Dialoge über Machtdynamiken und Design als Instrumente des Widerstands. Musiker*innen, Künstler*innen, Theoretiker*innen und andere Kreative nutzten diesen Ort als Ausgangspunkt für ihre Untersuchungen zu den sozialen und politischen Einflüssen von Denkmalen und Denkmälern weltweit.

In Saaleck wie überall auf der Welt sind Denkmale zu einem Brennpunkt der öffentlichen Debatte und des Aktivismus geworden, da Communities mit Fragen der Repräsentation, der Erinnerungskultur und der Identität ringen. Letztlich liegt die Bedeutung von Denkmalen nicht nur in ihrer physischen Präsenz, sondern auch in den Gesprächen und Aktionen, die sie auslösen. Indem sie sich mit Denkmalen und umstrittenen Orten auseinandersetzen, bieten Gesellschaften sich selbst die Gelegenheit, schwierigen Wahrheiten ins Auge zu blicken, dominante Narrative infrage zu stellen und auf eine gerechtere und gleichberechtigte Zukunft hinzuarbeiten. Das ist notwendig und bildet den Kern der Vision der dieDAS.

GEDÄCHTNIS IST IMPULS

Bryan C. Lee, Jr.

**NOMA, AIA, Gründer/Design Principal of Colloqate
und Design-Justice-Aktivist**

Kurz nach Mittag am 16. August 1960 erreichte ein Brief den neuen Eigentümer eines Hauses in Hamilton Township, New Jersey, in den USA. Das Viertel galt damals als rein weißer Bezirk und hatte dementsprechend das Prädikat C der Federal Housing Authority (dem zuständigen Bundesministerium), was bedeutete, dass es sich um eine mittelmäßige Gegend nahezu ohne Schwarze oder Braune Bewohner beziehungsweise Bewohnerinnen handelte. Der Drohbrief war von anonymen Nachbarn verfasst und adressiert an Roderick Woodard, einen 46-jährigen Postangestellten, einem Schwarzen Mann mit vier Kindern, der zu jener Zeit versuchte, sich ein besseres Leben aufzubauen. Roderick erhielt den Brief weniger als einen Monat nach dem Kauf des Hauses. In jenen wenigen Wochen der Eigentümerschaft wurde sein Besitz mit rassistischen Graffiti verunstaltet, sah er mehrere brennende Kreuze und wurde schließlich zum Ziel eines Brandanschlags. Roderick war mein Urgroßvater.

Damals wie heute sehen sich Schwarze Menschen häufig ähnlichen Herausforderungen ausgesetzt, wenn es darum geht, bezahlbare Häuser in sicheren Bezirken zu finden. Die Immobilienfirma äußerte Roderick gegenüber keinerlei Bedenken hinsichtlich der Nachbarn. Leider suchten ebenjene Nachbarn jedoch fast unverzüglich Vergeltung für den Verkauf. Dreißig Tage nach dem Erwerb eines neuen Zuhauses sah sich mein Urgroßvater mit der Ungerechtigkeit konfrontiert, die tief in all unseren nationalen Systemen verwurzelt ist, ob diese nun sozialstaatlicher, politischer, wirtschaftlicher oder aber räumlicher Natur sind.

Das traditionellerweise rassistische Sozialsystem betrachtete ihn als weniger würdig, geachtet und als Mensch behandelt zu werden. Das politische System stellte sicher, dass diese Überzeugungen ihren Weg in die rassistischen Kredit- und Hypothekenregularien und letztendlich Eingang in die bundespolitische Gesetzgebung zum sogenannten Redlining fanden. Dabei handelte es sich um eine Politik, nach der in bestimmten Gebieten gewisse Dienstleistungen nicht oder nur stark überteuert angeboten wurden. Dieses Wirtschaftssystem förderte die unterschiedliche Bewertung von Land und Eigentum auf der Grundlage von Zugehörigkeit zu ethnischen Gruppen und gesellschaftlichen Klassen. Das räumliche System der Rassentrennung verwendete die Grenzlinien von Land und Besitz zur anschließenden Durchsetzung der Rechtswirksamkeit sämtlicher übriger Systeme.

Dies ist nur eine von unzähligen ähnlichen Geschichten, aber doch eine, die es wert ist, erinnert zu werden, weil sie uns einen Einblick in die Strukturen einer Welt gewährt, die wir selbst geschaffen haben. Ich bin davon überzeugt, dass es für nahezu jede Ungerechtigkeit in der Welt eine Architektur gibt, einen Plan und ein Design, die sie aufrechterhält.

Meine Arbeit setzt sich dafür ein, die Privilegien und Machtstrukturen abzubauen, die Architektur und Design als Werkzeuge der Unterdrückung verwenden. Sie verdeutlicht die Rolle der Architektur bei der Schaffung von Räumen der Befreiung auch durch die Erzählungen von Menschen, Orten und Machtstrukturen, die allesamt sehr viel häufiger nebeneinander vorkommen, als dass dies ein Zufall sein könnte.

Ideologien der Unterdrückung aufrechtzuerhalten, hängt von der Fähigkeit einer Gesellschaft ab, ein kollektives Narrativ zu konstruieren, diese Überzeugungen in den Infrastrukturen zu verankern, die unsere Welt formen, und folglich alle Spuren alternativer Kulturen, Geschichten und Werte auszulöschen.

Wenn wir uns selbst die Geschichte erzählen, dass manche Menschen bestimmter Immobilien eher würdig sind als andere, dann schaffen wir Immobilienmärkte, die Menschen künstlich an der Armutsgrenze halten, während wir Wohnungs- und Obdachlosenkrisen fördern. Wenn wir uns die Geschichte erzählen, dass unsere Communities voneinander abgeschieden leben sollten, dann bauen wir Bezirke, Wohnungen, Straßen, Läden und Schulen, die eine solche Trennung bestätigen.

Wenn wir uns erzählen, dass manche Menschen gefährlicher sind als andere, dann schaffen wir Polizeisysteme, die nur der Gefängnisindustrie dienen, und diese wird nur dadurch aufrechterhalten, dass Räume entstehen, die wiederum das soziale und ökonomische Potenzial marginalisierter Gruppen abschöpfen. Wenn wir uns einreden, dass unsere Umwelt nicht unter den Auswirkungen unserer Gegenwart leidet, dann fahren wir damit fort, Bodenschätze aus der Erde zu extrahieren, unsere Wälder übermäßig auszubeuten und Gebäude zu bauen, die einen übermäßigen und untragbar großen Anteil an der Weltenergieproduktion erfordern.

Wenn wir uns diese Geschichten erzählen, werden unsere kollektiven Werte durch die Räume und Orte, die wir gestalten, bestätigt. Wir müssen erkennen, dass die Räume, die wir innerhalb rassistischer Systeme bauen, Denkmale für den Hochmut weißer Überlegenheit sind.

Die Wucht dieser Fragestellungen mag unüberwindlich erscheinen, doch die Erinnerungen, die wir bewahren, und die Sammlung von Erinnerungen, die wir als Reaktion auf die herrschenden Verhältnisse zusammentragen, werden die Welten definieren, die wir in Zukunft bauen. Wenn die Wurzel aller Unterdrückung im Verlust von Erinnerung besteht, dann muss die Wurzel aller Befreiung die unablässige Bewahrung und Schaffung von Erinnerung sein – in Sprache, in Geschichten, in Orten und in der Kultur.

Die Praxis der Design Justice glaubt daran, dass die Sprache, die wir verwenden, wenn wir die Geschichten von Orten erzählen, von wesentlicher Bedeutung ist. Architektur ist eine Sprache. Wie alle Sprachen ermöglicht sie uns, komplexe Erzählungen zu speichern, die in der Lage sind, die Bedeutung all unserer Geschichten so zu ehren, wie sie es verdienen.

Geschichten prägen sich in Orte ein – in unsere Bezirke, unsere Straßen, unsere Häuser – und verwandeln Erinnerung in Denkmale, denn Orte prägen unsere Alltagserfahrungen ebenso wie jene kulturellen Narrative, deren Fortbestehen wir zulassen.

Für Farbige Communities in Amerika existiert Macht in den Orten und Räumen, an denen unsere Kultur anerkannt wird, wo unsere Geschichten erzählt werden, wo unsere Sprache geschätzt wird. Wie die Griots in Mali, Westafrika, ist die gebaute Umgebung ein Archiv, ein Zeuge von Ungleichheit und Ungerechtigkeit, Freude und Widerstandsfähigkeit, Schmerz und Lust. Sie ist eine Geschichtenerzählerin, ein Licht auf unserem Weg durch eine unbarmherzige Welt. Es heißt, wenn ein Griot stirbt, brennt eine Bibliothek nieder.

Die Schwere dieser Metapher hat mich stets in der einfachen Vorstellung geerdet, dass Erinnerung ein Impuls ist. Das Gedächtnis treibt uns kollektiv an, erlaubt es Worten, durch Zeit und Sprache zu reisen, und stützt sich auf unsere Vernetzung in der Community, um bedeutungslosen Symbolen Sinn einzuhauchen und leblosen Räumen wieder Leben zu geben. Ohne sie treten wir unweigerlich auf der Stelle.

Architekt*innen, Planer*innen und Stadtentwickler*innen sind dafür verantwortlich, den kontinuierlichen Dialog zwischen der kulturellen Vielschichtigkeit eines Ortes und der architektonischen Sprache dieses Ortes zu interpretieren und zu übersetzen und dadurch die Mythologien in unserem Gedächtnis weiterleben zu lassen.

Darin liegt die grundlegende Aufforderung von Design Justice. Diese Fragen sind an sich schon vielschichtig, doch die kombinierten Auswirkungen auf marginalisierte Communities sind oftmals schlicht unerträglich. Unsere Arbeit zielt darauf ab, Räume sozialer, kultureller und wirtschaftlicher Gerechtigkeit als Akt der Reparation und der Heilung zu entwerfen.

Wenn ich eines festhalten möchte: Die Werte, die wir in unseren sozialen Konstrukten verkörpern, werden zu den Werten, die in den von uns errichteten Bauten verankert sind. Kunst und Architektur unserer gebauten Umgebung sind untrennbar mit unserer sozialen Existenz verknüpft. Doch die Tiefe dieser Beziehung ist im heutigen Diskurs über Rassismus und Unterdrückung noch immer von peripherer Bedeutung.

Letztendlich sehe ich Design als Werkzeug des Protests. Zu protestieren heißt, einen unbeugsamen Glauben an die Macht und das Potenzial zu haben, eine gerechte Gesellschaft zu bauen. Es geht im Kern um eine kollektive Hoffnung auf eine gemeinsame Zukunft, angetrieben von einer gemeinsamen Geschichte. Im besten Fall ist Design die physische Manifestation unseres kollektiven Gedächtnisses, die sich für eine gerechtere und befreite Welt einsetzt.

Dieser Essay ist ein Auszug aus Bryan C. Lees Publikation *Power + Place*, die sich in Vorbereitung befindet.

HEILIGTÜMER DER FÜRSORGE IN UNSICHEREN ZEITEN

Meriem Chabani

Partner bei TXKL und Präsidentin von The New South

Der Globale Norden reserviert wenig Raum für das Heilige. Inmitten seiner nunmehr Jahrhunderte andauernden Hegemonie erleben wir täglich eine durch Kapital geprägte Welt. Kapital ist die treibende Kraft, die unsere Städte, unser Zuhause und unser Alltagsleben formt. Reichtum und ungebremstes Wachstum werden höher bewertet als alles andere, was uns in eine Epoche geführt hat, in der Ungleichheit grassiert, gesellschaftlicher Aufruhr zunimmt und wir einer existenziellen Klimakrise gegenüberstehen. Wie können wir ein gleichwertiges und zugleich humaneres Wertesystem aufbauen, das einer solch mächtigen, zerstörerischen Kraft die Stirn bieten kann? Wie kann die Ehrung des Heiligen – des Unantastbaren – uns helfen, eine bessere Welt zu schaffen?

Die Künstlerin, Schriftstellerin, Aktivistin und Architekturforscherin Imani Jacqueline Brown untersucht das Vermächtnis von Plantagen und die Spuren, die die versklavte Bevölkerung entlang des Mississippi in Louisiana in den USA hinterließ. Dieses Gebiet hat sich von einem „Plantagenland" zu einem „petrochemischen Korridor" gewandelt, der heute auch als „Krebs-Allee" bekannt ist. Die brutalen Zuckerrohrfarmen wurden durch umweltzerstörende petrochemische Industrieanlagen ersetzt, was zu extrem hoher Luftverschmutzung mit toxischen Stoffen und einer der höchsten Krebsraten des Landes geführt hat. Die dort lebenden Schwarzen Communities sind über Generationen die Leidtragenden dieser Entwicklung gewesen.

Im Zentrum von Browns Forschung stehen Friedhöfe, die während der Untersuchungen für eine geplante Raffinerieerweiterung entdeckt wurden. Sie gehören vermutlich zu den Hunderten, wenn nicht Tausenden verborgenen Stätten der Ahnen, die von Entweihung bedroht sind. In Zusammenarbeit mit der Aktivistengruppe RISE St. James und dem Forschungslabor Forensic Architecture haben Browns Bemühungen krasse Beispiele für Umweltrassismus – ein direktes Erbe des Kolonialismus und der Sklaverei – ans Licht gebracht. Sie plädieren dafür, noch mehr Friedhöfe zu finden und ein Moratorium für die weitere Expansion der petrochemischen Industrie zu erlassen.[1] Dieser wiedergewonnene heilige Raum, der die Zeiten überdauert hat, legt schonungslos die Diskrepanz zwischen zwei widersprüchlichen Wertesystemen offen: einem, das von Kapital angetrieben wird, und einem anderen, das von Fürsorge geprägt ist.

Unterdessen bietet der Philosoph Mohamed Amer Meziane in seinem 2021 erschienenen Sachbuch *The States of the Earth* (frz. Orig.: *Des empires sous la terre*) eine Interpretation der Säkularisierung Europas im 19. Jahrhundert, die sowohl den vorherrschenden Rassismus als auch ökologische Aspekte betont. Er zieht eine Parallele zwischen der Loslösung von religiösen beziehungsweise spirituellen Belangen und dem Aufstieg des kolonialen kapitalistischen Extraktivismus, des Neoliberalismus und der Deregulierung. Mit dem Begriff des „Säkularozän" argumentiert er, dass der Boden unter unseren Füßen – zusammen mit seinen reichen Bodenschätzen – jede Verbindung zum transzendenten Göttlichen verloren hat. Dies geschah, als der Glaube an die himmlische Herrschaft über die Erde durch materialistische, imperialistische Ideologien ersetzt wurde, was die Erde einer grenzenlosen Kommerzialisierung und Ausbeutung überließ. Oder, um es mit den Worten von Meziane zu sagen: „Es ist die Kritik des Himmels, die die Erde erschüttert hat."[2]

In meiner eigenen Arbeit möchte ich erforschen, wie sich traditionelle, sakrale Praktiken in der gebauten Umwelt manifestieren und bewahren lassen, um innovative und vergessene nachhaltige Ansätze in der Architektur und Stadtplanung zu verwirklichen. Angesichts tiefgreifender, miteinander verknüpfter sozialer und ökologischer Krisen besteht die dringende Notwendigkeit, eine erneuerte Vision einer fortschrittlichen Modernität zu kultivieren. Wir brauchen sozusagen einen Heiligen Grünen New Deal.

Um das Heilige zu definieren, müssen wir über die Religion hinausdenken und uns stattdessen auf Fürsorge konzentrieren: Was haben Menschen über Zeiten und Zusammenhänge hinweg geschützt und gepflegt? Was sollte unberührt und unbefleckt, unangetastet bleiben? Wir müssen beginnen, die Existenz heiliger Praktiken weltweit anzuerkennen. Von Standing Rock bis zum brasilianischen Amazonas führen indigene Völker schon lange einen Kampf gegen extraktive und zerstörerische Landausbeutung . Melissa K. Nelson, eine Ökologin, indigene Wissenschaftlerin und Aktivistin, setzt sich für die Wiederherstellung indigener Verwaltung von Land und Wasser ein. „Wir indigenen Völker haben die kulturelle und spirituelle Verpflichtung, die indigenen Ideale der Wechselbeziehungen zu verkörpern und das Gleichgewicht zwischen Mensch und Ort wiederherzustellen",[3] betont sie. In dieser Hinsicht verfügt der Globale Süden über bedeutende Ressourcen, die uns dabei helfen können zu verstehen, wie Heiligkeit und gebaute Umwelt ineinandergreifen und florieren können.

Ein Beispiel dafür findet sich in der algerischen Wüste, in der Oasenstadt Ghardaia. Vor einigen Jahrzehnten beschlossen die Einwohner, ihre Siedlung über die historischen Stadtmauern hinaus zu erweitern und den umliegenden Palmenhain abzuholzen, um Platz für neue Häuser zu schaffen. Im Jahr 2008 führten starke Regenfälle zu einer katastrophalen Überschwemmung, die Hunderte von Häusern zerstörte und Dutzende von Menschen das Leben kostete. Die Nachbarstadt Beni Isguen, die ihren Baumbestand bewahrt hatte, war von den sintflutartigen Regenfällen weit weniger betroffen. Die Menschen in Ghardaia und in der gesamten Region erkannten den gravierenden Unterschied und stellten ihre fundamentale Beziehung zur Palme und deren wichtige Rolle beim Schutz ihrer Gemeinschaften wieder her.[4] Die Palme galt, wenn nicht als heilig, so doch zweifellos als ein Objekt von sakraler Bedeutung. Ihre Sakralisierung wurde hier mit relativem Erfolg für die Pflege von Naturreservaten eingesetzt. Doch die Geschichte von Ghardaia lehrt noch etwas Weiteres: Die Errichtung eines Heiligtums bedeutet nicht zwangsläufig eine Loslösung von der städtischen Landschaft; vielmehr unterstreicht sie die Notwendigkeit der Vernetzung. Heilige Stätten zu errichten, ist eine Methode, kollektiv Prioritäten zu definieren, die als absolut angesehen werden sollen.

Die Sakralisierung gewinnt weltweit an Zugkraft durch Bewegungen wie die 30×30-Initiative, eine internationale Koalition, die sich dem Ziel verschrieben hat, bis zum Jahr 2030 30 % der Land- und Meeresflächen der Erde unter staatlichen Schutz zu stellen.[5] Aus dieser Perspektive wird das Heilige nicht nur als umwelt- und sozialverträgliches, sondern auch als wirtschaftliches Prinzip verstanden: Das Heilige ist – sozusagen von seinem Design her – das, was über die Reichweite des zeitlichen, wirtschaftlichen Austauschs hinausgeht. In die Sprache der zeitgenössischen Architektur übersetzt, entzieht sich das Heilige dem Zugriff der unkontrollierten Immobilienentwicklung und der unbegrenzten, nicht tragbaren, sicher nicht nachhaltigen materiellen Ausbeutung.

Die Große Moschee von Djenné in Mali steht beispielhaft für kollektive Fürsorge in der Sahara. Alle Mitglieder der Gemeinde von Djenné beteiligen sich an der jährlichen Renovierung des historischen Lehmbaus, indem sie den Lehmboden vorbereiten und auftragen, um der starken Erosion entgegenzuwirken.[6] Durch die von Generation zu Generation weitergegebene kollektive Fürsorge wird die Heiligkeit der Moschee immer wieder als Eckpfeiler der städtischen Identität festgeschrieben und vereint ihre Bürger rund um ein zentrales Projekt. Die gemeinschaftliche Pflege des Gebäudes eröffnet neue Möglichkeiten für nachhaltige Praktiken in der gebauten Umwelt.

Auf der ganzen Welt bieten Fallbeispiele des Heiligen wertvolle Anleitungen, wie wir die verloren gegangene Verbindung zueinander und zur Erde wiederherstellen können. Die Wiedereinsetzung dieser Kosmogonien kann uns helfen, uns in der Ära des Säkularozän zurechtzufinden. Indem wir Heiligtümer wiederaufbauen, heilige Bündnisse zwischen Menschen und Orten erneuern und wirklich nachhaltige Städte pflegen, brechen wir aus unfruchtbaren Gefilden aus.

1. Imani Jacqueline Brown, Samaneh Moafi und Forensic Architecture zusammen mit RISE St. James, *Environmental Racism in Death Alley, Louisiana: Phase I Investigative Report*, 4.7.2021, https://content.forensic-architecture.org/wp-content/uploads/2021/07/Environmental-Racism-in-Death-Alley-Louisiana_Phase-1-Report_Final_2021.07.04.pdf (24.4.2024).
2. Mohamed Amer Meziane, *The States of the Earth: An Ecological and Racial History of Secularization*, übersetzt von Jonathan Adjemian, London 2024 (Originalausgabe: *Des empires sous la terre. Histoire écologique et raciale de la sécularisation*, Paris 2021).
3. Melissa K. Nelson, „Time to Indigenize Conservation: Native American Activists Are Leading a Push to Embed Traditional Ecological Knowledge in Land Management Decisions", 22.12.2020, in: *Sierra* (Januar/Februar 2021), https://www.sierraclub.org/sierra/2021-1-january-february/feature/time-indigenize-lands-and-water-conservation (26.4.2024).
4. UNESCO World Heritage Convention, Climate Change Case Studies, „Promoting Traditional Environmental Knowledge in the M'Zab Valley (Algeria)", https://whc.unesco.org/en/canopy/mzab/ (24.4.2024).
5. Eric Dinerstein u. a., „A Global Deal for Nature: Guiding Principles, Milestones, and Targets", *Science Advances*, 19.4.2019, https://www.science.org/doi/10.1126/sciadv.aaw2869 (24.4.2024).
6. The Children's Museum of Indianapolis, „The Great Mosque of Djenné, in: *Sacred Places*, https://sacredplacesexhibit.org/mali/ (24.4.2024); Jehan Alfarra, „Discover the Great Mosque of Djenné, Mali", in: *MEMO Middle East Monitor*, 4.7.2021, https://www.middleeastmonitor.com/20210704-discover-the-great-mosque-of-djenne-mali/ (24.4.2024).

RÄUME UND IDEOLOGIEN DER UNGLEICHHEIT IN DER KLIMAKRISE

Prof. Dr. Matthias Quent

Professor für Soziologie für die Soziale Arbeit,
Hochschule Magdeburg-Stendal

Es ist wunderbar, dass die Design Akademie Saaleck, an der Altes und Neues so präsent ist, Neues schafft. Hier, zwischen Wald, Bergen und dem Fluss Saale, etwas abseits der Zentren der Moderne und doch verkehrsgünstig gelegen, wirkte Paul Schultze-Naumburg vor 100 Jahren. Schultze-Naumburg, der zum hetzenden Rassisten und Antisemiten wurde, organisierte um die Jahrhundertwende den „Bund Heimatschutz". Dieser setzte sich nicht nur für den regionalen Natur- und Umweltschutz ein, sondern verstand sich als entschiedener Gegner industriellen Fortschritts.

Seine Mitglieder sahen den kapitalistischen Industriestaat als Bedrohung nicht nur für die heimische Natur, sondern auch für die deutsche nationale Identität und die deutsche Volksseele. In der heutigen extremen Rechten wird Schultze-Naumburg als einer der genuin rechten Ökologen positiv erwähnt. Um die Jahrhundertwende kämpfte er unter anderem gegen die industrielle Nutzung des Flusses Rhein für ein großes Wasserkraftwerk. Sicherlich würde er sich heute gegen Windkraftanlagen aussprechen. Und sicherlich würde er, der den „Kulturbolschewismus" und den Modernismus bekämpfte, die Vielfalt der Design Akademie und dieser Konferenz verachten. Mit dem Ort gehen die Verantwortung und die Möglichkeit einher, das Verhältnis von Faschismus, Umwelt, Raum und Modernisierung neu zu vermessen.

Die Tatsache, dass 100 Jahre nach dem Nationalsozialismus Rechtsextremisten in Europa und Nordamerika immer noch und wieder Menschen als „Kulturmarxisten" beschimpfen, angreifen und sogar ermorden, stellt die viel gepriesene Aufarbeitung der Vergangenheit infrage. Erschreckend an den alten Texten von Schultze-Naumburg ist nicht in erster Linie sein Rassismus, sondern die Aktualität der Diskursmuster eines oft kulturell begründeten Rassismus, der auch heute noch nicht nur in der extremen Rechten, sondern auch in der Mitte der Gesellschaft zu finden ist.

Schultze-Naumburg gehörte zu jenen Intellektuellen, die nicht nur wegen ihres extremen Rassismus und ihrer aktiven Unterstützung des NS-Regimes Verantwortung für den Massenmord an Jüdinnen und Juden, Nicht-Weißen, Homosexuellen, Sinti und Roma, Kranken und Behinderten, Linken, Künstlerinnen und Künstlern, Intellektuellen und anderen tragen. Schultze-Naumburg vertrat eine ökologisch, kulturell und rassisch begründete Lesart des ideologischen Kulturpessimismus der sogenannten Konservativen Revolution, deren Bedeutung – folgt man dem Historiker Fritz Stern – im Verhältnis zu den von den Deutschen begangenen Gräueltaten oft unterschätzt wird. Die Konservativen Revolutionäre, an denen sich viele europäische neofaschistische Intellektuelle und Agitatoren orientierten, beklagten immer wieder den Niedergang und Verfall, die Zerstörung von Kultur und Tradition oder, wie Schultze-Naumburg, die Veränderungen und Schädigungen der Umwelt durch die Moderne – Veränderungen, wie sie durch Urbanisierung und neue Raumnutzungen deutlich werden.[1] Die Konservativen Revolutionäre, die als Wegbereiter des Nationalsozialismus gelten, kritisierten die liberale Demokratie dafür, dass sie die vermeintlich natürliche Ungleichheit von Menschengruppen verleugne und auflöse. Die Nazis setzten diese Ungleichheit später mit brachialer Gewalt durch.

Ungleichheit war und ist der Kern des Rechtsextremismus. Schultze-Naumburg schrieb, es sei ein Fehler, dass die Arbeiterklasse „die falsche Doktrin von der Gleichheit der Menschen übernommen" habe. In Wirklichkeit sei nichts ungleicher als die Menschen, und diese Ungleichheit könne nicht durch Umwelteinflüsse beseitigt werden. 1928 hielt er fest: „Die Auslese zum Zwecke der Anpassung an die Umwelt ist leider bisher kaum bewusst angewandt worden",[2] womit er der Vernichtung unter ökologischen Vorwänden Vorschub leistete.

Der Hauptfeind der Faschisten war der Liberalismus, mindestens gleichauf mit dem Sozialismus. Eine zentrale Brückenideologie dafür nimmt der Antisemitismus in der Tradition des christlichen Antijudaismus ein.

Auch heute noch richten sich Gegenbewegungen gegen Gleichheit und Gerechtigkeit, insbesondere in den Bereichen Rasse, Geschlecht und Klasse. Je offensichtlicher die Substanzlosigkeit der Vorwände zur Rechtfertigung von Ungleichheit war, ist und bleibt, desto aggressiver und irrationaler beharren ihre Befürworter und Profiteure auf ihrer Durchsetzung. Verschwörungsnarrative, die meist antisemitisch strukturiert sind, sind Ausdruck dieser Radikalisierung. Die Pseudotheorien der menschlichen Rassen, die industrielle Vernichtung, der räumliche Imperialismus und der Zweite Weltkrieg sind das Ergebnis dieser Ideologien.

Der autoritär-nationalistische und meist antisemitische Kampf gegen die Moderne war jedoch nie ein Kampf gegen die Nutzung der modernen Technik für die eigene Sache. Vom Volksempfänger über den Volkswagen und V2-Raketen bis hin zu den heutigen sozialen Medien und zur Künstlichen Intelligenz haben faschistische Bewegungen stets Pionierarbeit bei der Instrumentalisierung moderner Technologien für politische Agitation geleistet.

Das Verhältnis von Rassismus und sozialem Raum im rechten Denken, das sich auch in ästhetischen Fragen ausdrückt, steht für einen auf Brutalität und Machtausübung beruhenden Herrschaftsanspruch. Die Gleichzeitigkeit von erstens romantischer Verklärung von Umwelt und Natur (bei Hitler vor allem der Berge), zweitens brachialer Stadtarchitektur zum Zwecke der Machtdemonstration und drittens industrieller Rationalität von Menschenvernichtungsanlagen und Kriegsproduktion zeigen, worum es wirklich ging: um die Beherrschung von Mensch und Natur. Dies entsprach dem totalen Anspruch des nationalsozialistischen Regimes, die vermeintliche Natürlichkeit der Hierarchien zwischen den Lebewesen in der Natur durch extreme Gewaltanwendung in der Welt der Menschen zu imitieren. Die faschistische Ökologie beruht nur vorgeblich auf der Auffassung, dass Mensch und Natur eins sind, sondern vielmehr auf der Überzeugung, dass die Politik die Rücksichtslosigkeit des Fressens und Gefressenwerdens in der Natur mit den Mitteln der industriellen Technologien imitieren muss – statt sie zur Verbesserung der Lebensbedingungen aller einzusetzen.

In Zeiten einer sich rasant verschärfenden Klimakrise werden die Stimmen des Ökofaschismus wieder lauter. In den USA, Neuseeland und Deutschland rechtfertigen rassistische Terroristen sogar ihre Gewalt mit ökofaschistischen Begriffen: Die Zahl der Nicht-Weißen müsse reduziert werden, um die weiße Rasse und ihre Heimat zu retten. Diese extremen ökofaschistischen Stimmen sind zwar eine Minderheit, aber sie verdeutlichen eine der Möglichkeiten, wie die eskalierende Krise ideologisch bewältigt werden kann, ohne eigene Privilegien infrage zu stellen.

Eine andere problematische Herangehensweise, die den antiökologischen Diskurs über die globale Erwärmung immer noch dominiert, ist die Leugnung ihrer Existenz, des menschlichen und industriellen Einflusses sowie die Veränderbarkeit des Klimawandels. Pseudostudien, gekaufte Experten, Angstmacherei, Desinformation und Verharmlosung des Klimawandels sind Teil der vorherrschenden Diskurse und Ideologien. Ähnlich wie sie einst gegen Demokratisierung und Industrialisierung waren, bekämpfen Rechtsradikale heute die Dekarbonisierung und den Multikulturalismus als vermeintlichen Untergang der Heimat, Nation, Wirtschaft und Kultur. Die Narrative der Verleugnung sind anschlussfähig, denn auch sie richten sich gegen Veränderungen, die als unbequem, teuer oder störend empfunden werden und die dem Gobalen Norden die Verantwortung für die Folgen der Industrialisierung vor Augen führen. Vor allem leiden unter diesen Folgen diejenigen am stärksten, die am wenigsten dazu beigetragen haben.

Auf einer strukturellen Ebene bedeutet Klimarassismus die Externalisierung der ökologischen Kosten des industriellen Wohlstands des mehrheitlich weißen Westens auf Kosten der mehrheitlich nicht-weißen Regionen und Menschen. Klimarassismus fungiert sowohl als Struktur wie auch als Mechanismus, der diese Strukturen reproduziert und legitimiert. Als globales Ungleichheitsprinzip prägt der Klimarassismus unsere tägliche Lebenswirklichkeit; er ist Teil der Alltagspraxis, die uns alle mit diesen Strukturen verbindet. Die Folgen von Kohlenstoffemissionen und Umweltschäden bei der Gewinnung von Rohstoffen bekommen vor allem diejenigen zu spüren, die ohnehin marginalisiert sind. Die statistisch schon heute am stärksten vom Klimawandel betroffenen Menschen und Gebiete sind arm, weiblich und BPoC.

Jedes Mal, wenn wir ein Windrad als ästhetisch störend empfinden oder uns über einen Trinkhalm aus Papier ärgern, sollten wir bedenken, dass dasselbe System, welches Milliarden Menschen Vorschriften für umweltfreundliches Verhalten auferlegt und Energie sowie Güter des täglichen Bedarfs teurer macht, einigen wenigen Superreichen ermöglicht, mit ihren Privatflugzeugen, Megayachten und ihrem Luxuskonsum in einer Woche mehr Kohlenstoff auszustoßen als der Durchschnittsbürger in seinem ganzen Leben. Die Superreichen stoßen tausendmal mehr Treibhausgase aus als der Durchschnittsbürger. Die reichsten 10 Prozent verursachen so viele Emissionen wie die ärmsten 50 Prozent der Weltbevölkerung. Wie kann das gerecht sein? Klimaschutz ist keine Frage des moralisch überlegenen Lebensstils, sondern eine Frage der sozialen Ungleichheiten.

Die Gegenreaktion auf das Verursacherprinzip ist Nationalismus. Es ist kein Zufall, dass viele der Staaten, deren Vergangenheit und Gegenwart von Kolonialismus, Industrialisierung und hohen Kohlenstoffemissionen geprägt sind und deren Eliten besonders von den globalen Ungleichheiten profitieren, in jüngerer Zeit starke rechtsautoritäre bis faschistische Bewegungen und Parteien hervorgebracht haben. Diese Bewegungen und Parteien teilen mindestens eine Gemeinsamkeit: die Verteidigung von Ungleichheiten. Dazu gehört der Widerstand gegen die Emanzipation von Frauen und nicht-binären Menschen, gegen die Gleichberechtigung von Migrantinnen und Migranten, gegen wirksamen Klimaschutz, gegen die Rechte indigener Bevölkerungsgruppen, gegen kritische Rassismusforschung und gegen eine echte Aufarbeitung der Vergangenheit. Dazu gehört auch die Abwehr gegen die Regulierung der Finanzmärkte und die Umverteilung von unten nach oben bei gleichzeitiger Ausrufung eines Kulturkampfes, in dem den Unter- und Mittelschichten eingeredet wird, sie seien die Opfer globaler, grüner oder angeblich „woker" Eliten. Dabei sind diese Schichten zugleich betroffene wie auch stabilisierende Bestandteile eines Regimes extremer Ungleichheit.

Ohne Klimagerechtigkeit ist eine demokratische Zukunft jedoch nicht denkbar. Dazu müssen sich Wirtschaft, Städte und Raumnutzung, Mobilität und Ernährung ändern, aber nicht für alle gleich stark. Wenn die Hauptverantwortlichen nur ein erträgliches Maß an Emissionen verantworten, muss sich die Mehrheit kaum verändern. In der Breite müssen wir vor allem den raumverschwendenden Überkonsum an Fleisch deutlich reduzieren. Klimagerechtigkeit muss sich konkret darin ausdrücken, dass die Reichen und Mächtigen, die Hauptverursacher der globalen Erwärmung, ihre Möglichkeiten nutzen, um die Armen, Schwachen und Machtlosen vor den zerstörerischen Folgen des Klimawandels zu schützen. Wir erleben jeden Tag, dass die meisten von ihnen dies nicht freiwillig tun und manche die Option des Faschismus in Erwägung ziehen, um ihre Privilegien zu verteidigen. Aber jede soziale und emanzipatorische Bewegung hat Fortschritte nur gegen Widerstände erkämpft.

Der Beitrag basiert auf dem Vortrag „Spaces and Ideologies of Inequality in the Climate Crisis" im Rahmen des walk + talk Symposiums der dieDAS am 2. September 2023 sowie auf dem Sachbuch *Klimarassismus. Der Kampf der Rechten gegen die ökologische Wende* (München 2022) von Matthias Quent, Christoph Richter und Axel Salheiser.

1. Fritz Stern, *Kulturpessimismus als politische Gefahr. Eine Analyse nationaler Ideologie in Deutschland*, Stuttgart 2018 (zuerst 1963).
2. Paul Schultze-Naumburg, *Kunst und Rasse*, München 1928, S. 315.

MONUMENTALE BEHARRLICHKEITEN UND KOMPLEXITÄTEN

Sarah M. Whiting

Dean und Josep Lluís Sert Professor of Architecture, Harvard University Graduate School of Design, und dieDAS Kuratoriumsmitglied

Das von Germane Barnes 2023 vorgegebene kuratorische Thema *Monumental Affairs: Leben mit umstrittenen Orten* zielt direkt auf eine Herausforderung, mit der sich die Architektur seit langem auseinandersetzt: Wie kann Design das einfangen und verkörpern, was ein Denkmal ausmacht? Wenn Denkmale als Speicher kollektiver Erinnerung verstanden werden, wie das Getty Research Institute mit seiner Ausstellung *MONUMENTality* im Jahr 2019 postuliert, wie würden sie dann wohl mit vielschichtigen, nuancierten oder umstrittenen Personen, Geschichtsauslegungen und Räumen umgehen?

Das Dilemma ist keineswegs neu. Im Jahr 1937 erklärte der Kulturkritiker Lewis Mumford das Denkmal für tot. Die Sterbesakramente spendete er ihm auf den Seiten der britischen Zeitschrift *CIRCLE*. Mumford setzte Denkmäler mit Grabsteinen gleich. Er betrachtete sie als Zeichen für etwas Stabiles, Konkretes und Totes, wohingegen die Moderne das Reich des Lebendigen ausmache, das Unmittelbare und das Nomadische. Mumford kam zu dem Schluss, dass „die bloße Vorstellung eines modernen Denkmals eine Contradictio in Termini ist: Wenn es ein Denkmal ist, kann es nicht modern sein, und wenn es modern ist, kann es kein Denkmal sein".[1]

Mumfords Text war ein Auszug aus seinem 1938 publizierten Manuskript *The Culture of Cities*. Das umfassendere Ziel, das er verfolgte, bestand darin, die Gesellschaft aus dem „toten" oder „paläotechnischen" Zeitalter der Industrialisierung in das von Mumford – in Anlehnung an Patrick Geddes – so genannte „biotechnische" Zeitalter zu führen. Dieses versprach eine Epoche der Flexibilität zu werden, die sich vom Mechanischen befreit und von der Physikalität der Vergangenheit löst.[2] Für Mumford bot das „Biotechnische" ein Gegenmittel zur Anomie der kapitalistischen Metropole. Es ermöglichte ein basisdemokratisches Modell der Partizipation, welches das Individuum in den Vordergrund stellte, das, so glaubte Mumford, durch die Bürokratisierung des industrialisierten Nationalstaats aus dem Blick verloren worden war. Mumfords flexible, „organische Körper" der Erneuerung bezogen ihre Kraft daraus, dass sie am Rande der Anarchie standen. Individualisierte Anarchie beziehungsweise das Risiko einer solchen verhinderte, dass die Demokratie von einer kapitalisti-

147

schen Bürokratie und einer zentralisierten Regierung vernichtet wurde.

Von derselben Annahme, dass nämlich das Denkmal, wie wir es kennen, tot ist, gingen auch die gerade in New York gelandeten europäischen Exilanten Sigfried Giedion, Josep Lluís Sert und Fernand Léger aus. Allerdings kamen sie 1943 zu einer gänzlich anderen Schlussfolgerung, als sie gemeinsam an einer Antwort auf die Aufforderung einer Gruppe namens American Abstract Artists arbeiteten, die sie jeweils um einen Beitrag zu einer geplanten Publikation gebeten hatte. Statt das Denkmal zu begraben, schlugen die drei Freunde seine Neuformulierung vor. Im Format eines avantgardistischen Manifests erstellten sie die so prägnanten wie polemischen „Neun Punkte über Monumentalität – ein menschliches Bedürfnis". Hierin umreißen sie ein Plateau für eine neue Form von Monumentalbau im Kontext der demokratischen US-amerikanischen Gesellschaft. Obwohl das Manifest erst 1956 erscheinen sollte (auf Deutsch; auf Englisch wurde es erst 1958 veröffentlicht), bildete es die Grundlage für Giedions weit verbreiteten Text mit dem Titel „A Need for a New Monumentality"[3] von 1944 einerseits und für den achten Congrès Internationale d'Architecture Moderne (CIAM) im Jahr 1951 im englischen Hoddesdon andererseits.

Zwar kamen Giedion, Sert und Léger zu einem anderen Schluss als Mumford, doch sie teilten seinen Glauben an Flexibilität, Leichtigkeit und Mobilität: „Bewegliche Elemente können das Aussehen der Bauten fortwährend verändern. Die beweglichen Elemente, veränderlichen Positionen und unterschiedlichen Schlagschatten können in Verbindung mit Wind oder Maschinen Quelle neuer architektonischer Effekte sein." Und genau wie Mumford war auch für Giedion, Sert und Léger der entscheidende Begriff, mit dem sie ihre polemische Schrift abschlossen, Freiheit: „In derartigen monumentalen Entwürfen könnten Architektur und Stadtplanung eine neue Freiheit gewinnen." Doch während Mumfords Freiheit die Freiheit des Individuums von den Fesseln der Mechanisierung war, ist die von Giedion, Sert und Léger die Freiheit des Ausdrucks „der kollektiven Kraft – der Menschen".

Mit anderen Worten hatten die Schrecken des Krieges bei den drei Europäern den Wunsch aufkeimen lassen, den kollektiven Ausdruck zu retten und wiederherzustellen. Giedions Augenmerk lag auf der Frage der kollektiven Subjektivität, also darauf, wie ästhetische Erfahrung eine kollektive Sinnlichkeit bestimmt. Nicht explizit in den „Neun Punkten" zu lesen, jedoch andernorts angedeutet, ist die Annahme, dass eine neue Politik und eine andere Wirtschaftsform von einer neuen Ästhetik hervorgebracht würden. In seinem Text „A Need for a New Monumentality" von 1944 schlägt Giedion etwa vor, dass die Architektur dem Aufruf des Wirtschaftswissenschaftlers John Maynard Keynes nach wirtschaftlicher Stimulierung folgen könnte: „Warum nicht Gemeindezentren bauen, um die Wirtschaft anzukurbeln?" Für die Frage, wie das Kriegsethos mit den Begriffen der Ästhetik zu vereinbaren sei, griffen Giedion, Sert und Léger die Frage der Monumentalität auf, um in einem bereits weit fortgeschrittenen Diskurs über die Fähigkeit zum Ausdruck im Rahmen der Moderne einzusteigen.

Was Mumford letztendlich von Giedion unterschied, war nicht so sehr eine Überzeugung für oder wider Monumentalität. Schließlich befürworteten beide eine Architektur und eine Stadtplanung, die mit ihrer jeweiligen Definition des Zeitgeists im Einklang stand. Die Unterschiede lagen vielmehr in ihren höchst verschiedenartigen Vorstellungen vom modernen Individuum und der Form des öffentlichen Raumes für dieses Individuum. Mumfords öffentliches Individuum beteiligt sich an einer kollektiven Erfahrung von bürgerlichen Symbolen, wohingegen Giedions kollektive Individuen sich mit einem öffentlichen Raum von abstrakt symbolischer Form auseinandersetzen.

Heute hinterfragt der Zeitgeist den Begriff des Denkmals radikal. Die Debatte in der Mitte des 20. Jahrhunderts über die Möglichkeit staatsbürgerlicher Symbolismen und ihre Auswirkungen auf singuläre beziehungsweise kollektive öffentliche Individuen wird dadurch weiter kompliziert, dass wir uns in einer Welt befinden, die nicht nur Denkmäler infrage stellt, sondern auch die Prämissen, die alten Definitionen kollektiver Subjektivität zugrunde liegen. Ein Artikel in der *Washington Post* beschrieb detailliert, dass zwischen 2015 und 2021 mehr als 140 Denkmäler für die Seite der Konföderierten im Amerikanischen Bürgerkrieg aus dem öffentlichen Raum entfernt wurden.[4] *The Guardian* schrieb von fast 70 Denkmälern für Kolonialisten und Sklavenhändler, die über einen ähnlichen Zeitraum im Vereinigten Königreich abgetragen wurden.[5] In seinem Artikel *Politico* zeigt der Historiker Joshua Zeitz auf, dass „im Jahr 1949, die Bundesrepublik Deutschland die Zurschaustellung von Hakenkreuzen unter Strafe gestellt hat. Das Nazi-Symbol wurde ebenfalls von Häusern entfernt, mitunter sogar abgesprengt. Die Bundesrepublik ließ systematisch Statuen und Denkmäler zerstören, riss zahlreiche vom Nazi-Regime errichteten Gebäude ab und begrub hingerichtete militärische wie zivile Vertreter*innen des Regimes in unmarkierten Massengräbern. So sollte dem Entstehen von Wallfahrtsorten für Nazis an ihren Gräbern vorgebeugt werden."[6]

Auf nationaler Ebene findet überall auf der Welt seit Jahrzehnten eine Neubewertung von Denkmälern, Personen und historischen Tatsachen statt. Dies steht auch im Fokus vieler Institutionen, darunter der Harvard University, die im April 2022 den *Report of the Presidential Committee on Harvard and the Legacy of Slavery* veröffentlichte. Die Vorstellung des Berichts wurde mit dem Versprechen begleitet, 100 Millionen US-Dollar für die Umsetzung seiner Empfehlungen bereitzustellen. Unter diesen Empfehlungen befand sich auch die Errichtung eines Denkmals: „Wir empfehlen der Universität, die versklavten Menschen, deren Arbeit die Gründung, das Wachstum und die Entwicklung von Harvard mit ermöglicht hat, durch ein dauerhaftes und imposantes physisches Denkmal, einen Versammlungsraum oder beides anzuerkennen und zu ehren."[7]

Zusammenfassend lässt sich beinahe 90 Jahre nachdem Lewis Mumford das Denkmal für tot erklärt hat, mit einiger Zuversicht sagen, dass es alles andere als tot ist. Wenn wir den Bogen zurück zu Germane Barnes' Apell zum Handeln, *Monumental Affairs: Leben mit umstrittenen Orten*, schlagen, so erscheint das von ihm gewählte Thema zugleich zeitlos und hochaktuell. Wie dieDAS begibt sich die Graduate School of Design (GSD) auf dieses nach wie vor vielschichtige Terrain, weil sie Geschichte nuanciert, sorgfältig und mit Tiefgang studiert, während sie gleichzeitig auch unsere Zukunft im Blick hat, mit Materialien experimentiert, Ressourcen untersucht sowie Wege erforscht, wie Menschen mit diversen Biografien zusammenleben und zusammenarbeiten können. Die Synergieeffekte zwischen unseren beiden Instituten wird durch die Anzahl der GSD-Absolvent*innen unterstrichen, die bereits dieDAS Fellows gewesen sind oder an den jährlich stattfindenden dieDAS walk + talk Symposien teilgenommen haben. Wir sehen der weiteren Kollaboration mit Freude entgegen, sobald das Architektenhaus restauriert und zu einem Standort für zukunftsweisende Forschung geworden ist.

1949 gab Mumford zu, dass Denkmäler vielleicht am ehesten durch Botschaften zu ersetzen seien: „Möglicherweise lässt sich Giedions These am besten so neu formulieren, dass es nicht ausreicht, wenn moderne Gebäude etwas sind oder etwas tun: Sie müssen auch etwas sagen. [...] moderne Architekten haben ihre Grammatik und ihr Vokabular gelernt und sind nun bereit zu sprechen."[8] Als Ort für Dialog, Forschung und Gestaltung wird dieDAS in Saaleck uns alle ins Gespräch bringen.

1. Lewis Mumford, „The Death of the Monument", in: J. L. Martin u. a. (Hrsg.), *CIRCLE: International Survey of Constructive Art*, London 1971 (zuerst 1937), S. 263–271, hier S. 264.
2. Freundlicherweise lieferte Mumford seinen Leserinnen und Lesern ein Lexikon für die Geddes' Neologismen: „PALÄOTECHNIK: Bezieht sich auf die Kohle- und Stahlwirtschaft [...]; NEOTECHNIK: Bezieht sich auf die neue Wirtschaft [...] die auf die Verwendung von Elektrizität beruht, auf Leichtmetallen, [...] und seltenen Metallen; BIOTECHNIK: Bezieht sich auf die im Entstehen begriffene Wirtschaft, die sich bereits vom neotechnischen (noch nicht rein mechanischen) Komplex absetzt und auf eine Zivilisation vorausweist, in der die biologischen Wissenschaften ungehemmt auf die Technik angewendet werden und in der die Technik selbst auf die Lebenskultur ausgerichtet sein wird. [...] In der biotechnischen Ordnung werden die Biologie und die Sozialwissenschaften tonangebend. [...] Fortschritte hängen nicht mehr ausschließlich von mechanischen Manipulationen von Materie und Energie ab, sondern werden vielmehr auf dem organischen Gebrauch der gesamten Umwelt beruhen. Dieser ist eine Reaktion auf die Bedürfnisse der Organismen und Gruppen hinsichtlich ihrer mannigfaltigen Beziehungen: physikalische, biologische, soziale, ökonomische, ästhetische und psychologische." Übersetzt nach: Lewis Mumford, *The Culture of Cities*, New York 1970 (zuerst 1938), S. 495f.
3. Deutsche Fassung: Sigfried Giedion, „Über eine neue Monumentalität" (1944), in: ders., *Wege in die Öffentlichkeit*, hrsg. von Dorothee Huber, Zürich 1987, S. 180–195.
4. Bonnie Berkowitz und Adrian Blanco, „A record number of Confederate monuments fell in 2020, but hundreds still stand. Here's where", in: *Washington Post*, 17.6.2020 (aktualisiert 12.3.2021); https://www.washingtonpost.com/graphics/2020/national/confederate-monuments/ (8.5.2024).
5. Aamna Mohdin und Rhi Storer, „Tributes to slave traders and colonialists removed across UK", in: *The Guardian* 29.1.2021; https://www.theguardian.com/world/2021/jan/29/tributes-to-slave-traders-and-colonialists-removed-across-uk (8.5.2024).
6. Joshua Zeitz, „Why There Are No Nazi Statues in Germany: What the South Can Learn from Postwar Europe", in: *Politico*, 20.8.2017; https://www.politico.com/magazine/story/2017/08/20/why-there-are-no-nazi-statues-in-germany-215510/ (8.5.2024).
7. „Recommendation: Honor Enslaved People through Memorialization, Research, Curricula, and Knowledge Dissemination", in: *Report of the Presidential Committee on Harvard & the Legacy of Slavery*, 26.4.2022; https://legacyofslavery.harvard.edu/report (8.5.2024).
8. Lewis Mumford, „Monumentalism, Symbolism and Style", in: *The Architectural Review*, April 1949, S. 173–180, hier S. 173.

DIE SAALECKER WERKSTÄTTEN ALS UNBEQUEMES ERBE

Daniela Spiegel

Prof. Dr.-Ing., Professur Denkmalpflege und Baugeschichte, Bauhaus-Universität Weimar

Im Laufe der vergangenen Jahrzehnte sind immer mehr Denkmale im öffentlichen Diskurs als umstritten deklariert worden. Mittlerweile stellen „unbequeme Denkmale" einen eigenen Forschungszweig in der Denkmaltheorie dar. Doch was genau sind eigentlich unbequeme Denkmale?

Bei der Annäherung an die Frage hilft zunächst eine genauere Beschäftigung mit den Begrifflichkeiten. Denkmale sind dem etymologischen Ursprung des Wortes (von lat. monere = erinnern, auf etwas aufmerksam machen) zufolge Objekte, die uns heute, in der Gegenwart, an etwas aus der Vergangenheit erinnern. Wenn die Objekte extra für diesen erinnernden Zweck geschaffen wurden, wie zum Beispiel Statuen, spricht man von „gewollten Denkmalen". Daneben gibt es aber auch „gewordene Denkmale": Sie fungieren als materielle Zeugen von etwas, was als erinnernswert betrachtet wird, und werden deshalb zu Denkmalen erklärt. Ein Denkmal ist demnach ein Träger von Werten, und das Identifizieren und Erläutern dieser Werte ist eine Kernaufgabe der Denkmalpflege. Zu den klassischen Werten, die in Deutschland auch in den Denkmalgesetzen festgeschrieben sind, gehören zum Beispiel die Erhaltungswürdigkeit aus historischen und künstlerischen, aber auch aus städtebaulichen, technischen oder volkskundlichen Gründen.

Während die meisten Denkmalwerte allein positiv konnotiert sind, als herausragende Leistungen in der jeweiligen Sparte, kann sich der historische Wert eines Objekts durchaus auch auf ein negatives Ereignis oder eine negativ konnotierte Person beziehen. Überdies sind die Wertzuschreibungen nicht statisch; sie können sich mit der Zeit verändern – nicht nur in Bezug auf ein Gebäude, sondern auch gesellschaftlich. Das funktioniert in beide Richtungen: Ehemals diskreditierte Gebäude können von nachfolgenden Generationen wieder geschätzt werden, und umgekehrt können Personen oder Ereignisse, zu deren Ehrung oder Erinnerung Denkmäler geschaffen wurden, von späteren Generationen ganz anders beurteilt werden.

Letzteres war und ist immer noch ein zentrales Thema im Bereich der gewollten Denkmale. Durch eine veränderte Sichtweise oder Infragestellung der bis dato gepflegten Erinnerungskultur können solche Denkmäler plötzlich unbequem werden – mitunter so unbequem, dass sie gestürzt beziehungsweise vom Sockel geholt werden. Über die adäquate oder „richtige" Art des Umgangs wird zumeist heftig gestritten – Denkmäler sind also auch Objekte gesellschaftlicher Aushandlungsprozesse.

Im Bereich der gewordenen Denkmale wird der Begriff des „Unbequemen" auf unterschiedlichen Ebenen verwendet. Einerseits benennt er bauliche Zeugnisse noch nicht lange zurückliegender Epochen, die von der Fachwelt bereits als Denkmale erkannt wurden, ohne dass darüber ein gesellschaftlicher Konsens besteht. Solche Bauten sind meist nur für eine Zeitspanne von circa 30 Jahren unbequem, bis sie genügend historisiert und somit auch allgemein akzeptiert werden.

Andererseits wird der Begriff für Erbe-Orte verwendet, über deren Erhalt es einen gesellschaftlichen Konsens gibt, die jedoch aufgrund ihrer Geschichte unbequem sind, wie beispielsweise Orte des Verbrechens. Wobei der Begriff „unbequem" hierfür mitunter zu schwach erscheint, denn manche Orte sind durch ihre Geschichte regelrecht kontaminiert. Eine andere als eine museale Nutzung als Mahnmal oder Lernort scheint daher kaum möglich.

Am denkmalpflegerisch wohl herausforderndsten sind jene Orte oder Objekte, bei denen das Unbequeme nicht offensichtlich ist und bei denen eine Nutzung über die reine Mahnung und Erinnerung hinaus möglich und/oder sinnvoll scheint. Für sie eine adäquate Funktion zu finden, die sich auch aktiv mit der unbequemen Vergangenheit auseinandersetzt, stellt stets eine große Herausforderung dar. Und so richtig unbequem wird es, wenn es eine starke Diskrepanz zwischen dem unbequemen Inhalt und der bequemen Form gibt, die ihn umgibt.

Zu letzteren gehören zweifelsohne die Saalecker Werkstätten, die sich Paul Schultze-Naumburg Anfang des 20. Jahrhunderts als eigenes Wohnhaus und bald auch als Firmensitz schuf. Das weitläufige Ensemble ist fantastisch gelegen: Kühn erheben sich die beiden Hauptgebäude, das Wohnhaus und das als Büro der Werkstätten genutzte sogenannte Architektenhaus, auf dem felsigen Bergsporn über der Saale-Schleife, mit weitem Blick über die hügelige Landschaft. Nach Osten wird es durch den Trakt der Wirtschaftsgebäude abgeschirmt, der in elegantem Schwung zum hoch aufragenden Torhaus führt. Zwischen ihnen erstrecken sich auf mehreren Ebenen terrassierte Gärten.

Obgleich seit Jahrzehnten leer stehend, strahlt der Ort noch immer die angenehme Ruhe eines Refugiums aus, an dem sich vorstellbar gut wohnen und arbeiten lässt. Kurzum: Der Ort selbst erscheint auf den ersten Blick eigentlich sehr bequem. Hinzu kommt: Hier sind keine schrecklichen Dinge geschehen (zumindest wissen wir nichts davon), und auch die Bauten, Interieurs und Gartengestaltungen, die in den hiesigen Werkstätten entworfen wurden, waren durchaus gängige Produkte für die damalige Ober- und Mittelschicht.

Es ist vielmehr die Ambivalenz des dahinterstehenden Masterminds – des Bauherrn, der in autodidaktischer Eigenregie den Ort mit allen Details persönlich entwarf und gestaltete –, welche die Saalecker Werkstätten zu einem unbequemen Erbe werden lässt. Paul Schultze-Naumburg ist in der Tat eine der schillerndsten und irritierendsten Persönlichkeiten der deutschen Kulturgeschichte der ersten Hälfte des 20. Jahrhunderts. Zu Beginn seiner Karriere war er durchaus ein Anhänger reformerischer Tendenzen. Er gehörte zu den Mitbegründern des Deutschen Werkbunds, der für modernes Produktdesign einstand, und war Gründungsmitglied des Deutschen Bundes Heimatschutz. Seine Kritik an den Auswüchsen der Industrialisierung und des Historismus äußerte er vor allem in der 1901 bis 1917 publizierten Reihe der Kulturarbeiten, mit denen er zu einem Vordenker des heute so wichtigen Konzepts der Kulturlandschaft wurde. Nach dem Ersten Weltkrieg jedoch wurde aus dem konservativen Reformer ein glühender Anhänger rassistisch-nationalsozialistischer Kulturpolitik, der gegen die künstlerische Avantgarde der Moderne kämpfte. Die ästhetische und politische Radikalisierung Schultze-Naumburgs gipfelte 1928 in der Buchpublikation *Kunst und Rasse*, in der er die diskreditierende Argumentation der „Entarteten Kunst" des Nationalsozialismus vorwegnahm. Bereits in den 1920er-Jahren waren Hitler, Goebbels und Himmler gern gesehene Gäste in Saaleck, Schultze-Naumburg selbst trat 1930 der Partei bei.

Die Saalecker Werkstätten wurden also von einem Menschen geschaffen, der nicht nur die rassistischen, nationalsozialistischen Ideen teilte, sondern sich aktiv an deren theoretischer Grundlagenbildung beteiligte. Seine Gedanken formte, diskutierte und verschriftlichte er genau an diesem Ort – im Arbeitszimmer, am Esstisch, auf der Terrasse. Das ist der Umstand, der das Ensemble zu einem unbequemen Erbe macht. Wenngleich auch nur auf der Theorieebene, ist und bleibt es damit ein Täterort.

Schultze-Naumburg wirkte nur bis 1930 in Saaleck; er gab die Werkstätten auf, als die NSDAP in die Thüringer Landesregierung einzog und ihn zum Direktor der Weimarer Kunsthochschule berief. In dieser Funktion sah er seine Aufgabe darin, die Schule nach den „Irrwegen des Bauhauses" wieder zu einer Ausbildungsstätte wahrer deutscher Architektur zu machen. Dieses nur knapp zehn Jahre zählende Direktorat wiederum ist ein unbequemes Erbe für diejenigen, die mit der heutigen Bauhaus-Universität Weimar verbunden sind, an der ich selbst das Privileg habe, zu lehren und zu forschen. Schultze-Naumburg ist ein festes Verbindungsglied zwischen Weimar und Saaleck – nicht nur in der Vergangenheit, sondern auch in der Gegenwart.

Die glückselige Wendung, die die Saalecker Werkstätten nach Jahrzehnten des Leerstands erfuhren, nahm ihren Anfang auf einer Tagung, die von Hans-Rudolf Meier und mir im Dezember 2015 an der Professur Denkmalpflege und Baugeschichte der Bauhaus-Universität in Weimar veranstaltet wurde. Dort präsentierten wir auch ein Semesterprojekt, in dem Studierende der Urbanistik und Architektur sich mit verschiedenen Aspekten des strittigen und unbequemen Erbes Schultze-Naumburgs und dem damals leerstehenden Ensemble in Saaleck beschäftigten und mögliche Nutzungsperspektiven aufzeigten.

Einer der interessierten Tagungsteilnehmer war Arne Cornelius Wasmuth, der sich davon inspirieren ließ und anschließend mit unglaublicher Verve des Ortes annahm. Dank ihm, der Marzona Stiftung Neue Saalecker Werkstätten und dem engagierten Team, mit dem sie zusammenarbeiten, wurde auf Basis des dieDAS-Konzepts für das Anwesen eine neue Funktion gefunden: Diese bewahrt nicht nur das bauliche Erbe denkmalgerecht, sondern nimmt sich auch aktiv des unbequemen inhaltlichen Erbes an und macht es in positiver Weise für die Gesellschaft nutzbar.

TRANSFORMATION EINES UNBEQUEMEN DENKMALS
Stephan Kujas
Denkmalpfleger Stadt Weißenfels

Im durch Weinanbau und Landwirtschaft geprägten Flusstal der Saale in Mitteldeutschland befindet sich unweit der Stadt Naumburg der kleine Ort Saaleck. In dieser landschaftlich reizvoll gelegenen Gegend wurde im Jahr 1903 unterhalb einer Burgruine aus dem Mittelalter ein herrschaftliches Landhaus- und Gartenensemble errichtet, das sich auf einem Felsen über dem Tal erhebt. Erbaut wurde der Komplex vom Maler, Architektur-Autodidakten, rassistischen Ideologen und völkischen Vordenker Paul Schultze-Naumburg (1869–1949), der hier zwischen 1903 und 1930 seinen Wohnsitz und den Sitz seines erfolgreichen Architektur-, Gartenbau- und Innenausstattungsunternehmens, der Saalecker Werkstätten, hatte.

Während seiner Zeit in Saaleck verfasste Schultze-Naumburg mit seinen Kulturarbeiten eine Reihe vielgelesener Abhandlungen über Kunst, Architektur, Geschmack und Naturbetrachtungen. Zweifelhafte Berühmtheit erlangte sein 1928 erschienenes Buch *Kunst und Rasse*, das auf seinen Vorstellungen einer völkischen Kunst basiert und in erster Linie zeitgenössische, moderne Kunst als „entartet" diffamieren sollte. In Bildgegenüberstellungen verwendete er in diesem Buch Werke der Moderne und stellte diesen Fotografien von Menschen mit Behinderungen und Missbildungen gegenüber, um seine Ausführungen zu stützen. In der Herabwürdigung von Menschen und Kunstwerken bereitete er damit den mörderischen Entwicklungen im nationalsozialistischen Deutschland den publizistischen Boden.

In Saaleck bildete sich in den 1920er-Jahren um Paul Schultze-Naumburg ein berüchtigter informeller Kreis von Nationalsozialisten (darunter sind Adolf Hitler, Joseph Goebbels und Heinrich Himmler belegt), die ihn als wichtigen Türöffner zum deutschen Bürgertum schätzten. Durch seine publizistische Reichweite, seine persönlichen Netzwerke und seine Popularität in der bürgerlichen Öffentlichkeit trug Schultze-Naumburg wesentlich dazu bei, der rassistischen Ideologie einen achtbaren Anstrich zu verleihen und sie für die Massen akzeptabel zu machen. Mit seinem Werk und seinem Wirken gehört er somit zu den frühen Wegbereitern der Nationalsozialisten.

Als Stätte der nationalsozialistischen Geistesgeschichte ist der Komplex der Saalecker Werkstätten heute ein unbequemes Denkmal, das für immer durch seine dunkle Geschichte geprägt sein wird. Auf den ersten Blick lassen Haus und Garten in Saaleck jedoch die rassistische und antisemitische Ideologie, die dort formuliert wurde, nicht erkennen. Die Vergangenheit liegt im Verborgenen und erschließt sich den Besucherinnen und Besuchern nicht ohne Weiteres. Daher muss eine differenzierte denkmalpflegerische und inhaltliche Auseinandersetzung mit dem Ort stattfinden, um diesen Hintergrund herauszuarbeiten und zugänglich zu machen. Dieser Aufgabe stellt sich derzeit die Marzona Stiftung Neue Saalecker Werkstätten.

2018 erwarb der Berliner Kunstsammler und Mäzen Egidio Marzona über die Marzona Stiftung Neue Saalecker Werkstätten das Wohnhaus und den Garten der ehemaligen Werkstätten mit dem Ziel, einen progressiven Lernort für Designer und Architekten zu schaffen. Hier sollen Ansätze für eine bessere, egalitäre und nachhaltige Zukunft erforscht und gleichzeitig der Diskurs über die Vergangenheit des Ortes gefördert werden.

Marzona formuliert den Auftrag der Stiftung wie folgt: „An diesem Ort, der uns an das dunkelste Kapitel unserer Geschichte erinnert, werden wir dem Schaden, den der rechtsextreme Populismus anrichtet, mit freiem Austausch begegnen. International ausgerichtet und weltoffen, werden wir den Boden für innovative Ideen bereiten." Mit der Umnutzung der Saalecker Werkstätten für neue produktive Nutzungen stellt sich die Stiftung bewusst dem unbequemen Denkmal, um ein deutliches und spürbares Zeichen für die Kraft des Wandels in einer demokratischen und offenen Gesellschaft zu setzen.

Dank der Förderung durch das Land Sachsen-Anhalt und die Beauftragte der Bundesregierung für Kultur und Medien laufen seit 2019 die Vorbereitungen für die Sanierung und den Umbau des Komplexes zur dieDAS – Design Akademie Saaleck. Neben zahlreichen Voruntersuchungen erarbeitete das Landesamt für Denkmalpflege und Archäologie Sachsen-Anhalt zunächst eine denkmalpflegerische Zielstellung, die als Leitlinie für die weitere Planung dient. Eine vollständige Restaurierung und Rekonstruktion des Saaleck-Komplexes im Sinne von Schultze-Naumburg kommt dabei nicht infrage.

Da sich die Marzona Stiftung vom Bauherrn und seinen Ideen distanziert, muss die Umgestaltung des Geländes der Saalecker Werkstätten und seine zeitgemäße Inwertsetzung einen zukunftsweisenden gestalterischen Ausdruck erhalten. Aus diesem Grund wurde 2020 ein beschränkter internationaler Wettbewerb ausgelobt, um Vorschläge für die Wiederherstellung und Neuausrichtung des Geländes durch die Anwendung einer einheitlichen Architektursprache auf alle neuen Bauelemente zu erhalten und gleichzeitig einen angemessenen Umgang mit der erhaltenen Substanz und ihren Zeitschichten zu formulieren. Der Ort wurde seit seiner Errichtung mehrfach umgebaut und umgestaltet, und die Spuren der Entwicklung, die noch vorhanden sind, sollten – zumindest in Ansätzen – erhalten werden. In einem jurierten Auswahlverfahren konnte sich die dänische Architektin Dorte Mandrup mit ihren Ideen für den gesamten Komplex durchsetzen. Der Siegerentwurf macht die Vergangenheit bis in die jüngste Zeit hinein sichtbar und fügt gleichzeitig eine zeitgemäße Haut aus neuen Materialien und Farben hinzu, die zukünftige Inhalte, Gedanken und Visionen ermöglicht.

Ein wesentlicher Bestandteil der Arbeit der Marzona Stiftung ist die Einrichtung eines Lern- und Dokumentationszentrums, das sich mit der antisemitischen und nationalsozialistischen Vergangenheit des Ortes und dem schwierigen Erbe seines Architekten auseinandersetzt. Das Zentrum wird sich in der Nähe des Torhauses befinden und nach seiner Fertigstellung dauerhaft für Besucherinnen und Besucher geöffnet sein. Parallel zu den geplanten Bauarbeiten läuft eine wissenschaftliche Aufarbeitung, deren Ergebnisse in ein analoges und digitales Ausstellungskonzept münden werden. Die zukünftige Ausstellung soll den reflektierten Umgang mit der Vergangenheit für die politische Bildungsarbeit produktiv machen und auf unterschiedliche politische und kulturelle Zeitfragen Bezug nehmen. Das Zentrum für Antisemitismusforschung (ZfA) der Technischen Universität Berlin hat im Auftrag der Stiftung bereits eine erste Konzeptskizze für die Dauerausstellung erstellt, an deren Umsetzung in weiteren Schritten gearbeitet wird.

Eine Medienstation, die ursprünglich im Dokumentationszentrum Topographie des Terrors in Berlin ausgestellt war und die antisemitischen Netzwerke von Schultze-Naumburg illustriert, ist bereits als Leihgabe in Saaleck zu sehen. Diese Medienstation ist ein Ergebnis des DFG-Kooperationsprojekts „Paul Schultze-Naumburg und die Ästhetik des Volkstums in Architektur und Gartenkultur" der Universität der Künste Berlin und der Technischen Universität Darmstadt. Um die Erkenntnisse aus diesem DFG-Projekt für das Lern- und Dokumentationszentrum nutzbar zu machen, wird derzeit eine gemeinsame Kooperation mit den federführenden Wissenschaftlern mit dem Zentrum für Antisemitismusforschung, der Landeszentrale für politische Bildung und dem Institut für Landesgeschichte Sachsen-Anhalt vorbereitet. Die Ergebnisse der wissenschaftlichen Begleitforschung werden schrittweise in den Aufbau der Ausstellung und in innovative Vermittlungsformate umgesetzt.

Ein weiterer Teil der Stiftungsaktivitäten wird die künstlerische Auseinandersetzung mit dem Ort als unbequemem Denkmal sein. Auf diese Weise werden individuelle Perspektiven und Erfahrungen mit der Geschichte der Saalecker Werkstätten und darüber hinaus aus der Perspektive internationaler Kreativschaffender erfahrbar.

Das Gelände der ehemaligen Saalecker Werkstätten ist für die Marzona Stiftung Neue Saalecker Werkstätten ein herausforderndes Erbe, das sie jedoch mit offenen Augen und klaren Zielen angetreten hat. Der Weg der Stiftung zur Rückgewinnung und Umgestaltung des Geländes wird ein kontinuierlicher Prozess sein, der sich durch die unterschiedlichen mit dem Ort beschäftigten Akteurinnen und Akteure entfaltet und entwickelt. Auf diese Weise werden die Saalecker Werkstätten in einen dynamischen und inklusiven Ort des freien Denkens, der Gestaltung, des Diskurses und des künstlerischen Ausdrucks verwandelt, der zugleich historisch verantwortlich und zukunftsorientiert ist.

AUSSTELLEN, LASSEN, HINZUFÜGEN
Dorte Mandrup
Architektin, Gründerin und Kreativdirektorin von
Dorte Mandrup

Wie verleiht man einem historisch belasteten Denkmal neue Bedeutung, ohne zugleich die Vergangenheit auszulöschen? In solchen Fällen eine feine Balance zu finden, ist ein äußerst kompliziertes Unterfangen. Diese Aufgabe ist komplex und erfordert ein gründliches Verständnis des Ortes, seiner Geschichte und der emotionalen Bedeutung, die er mit sich bringt. So lassen sich strategische, sensible Interventionen unternehmen, die es zukünftigen Generationen ermöglichen, sich mit ebendieser Historie auseinanderzusetzen und gleichzeitig die Entwicklung von neuen Bewegungen und Werten zu fördern. Als Architekt*innen ist es unsere Aufgabe, neue Wege zu finden, um eine positive Einstellung zu verankern, indem wir die Vergangenheit kommentieren, sie entlarven und ihr die Macht nehmen – sie unschädlich machen.

An einen Felsen hoch über dem Fluss Saale geschmiegt, blicken die Saalecker Werkstätten zurück auf eine schwerwiegende und vielschichtige Vergangenheit, die unwiderruflich mit dem Architekten und rassistischen Ideologen Paul Schultze-Naumburg verknüpft ist, der als einer der führenden Vertreter der nationalsozialistischen Kulturpolitik bekannt wurde. Während der 1920er-Jahre entwickelte sich der Gebäudekomplex – sonst relativ neutrale Räumlichkeiten in wunderschöner Hügellandschaft – zu einer Hochburg nationalsozialistischen Gedankenguts und letztendlich einem Think-Tank für totalitäre und rassistische Ideologie. Der Ort bringt eine schwierige und verstörende Geschichte mit sich, die weder ignoriert noch vergessen werden darf, aber dennoch die Kreativität und die Ideale kommender Generationen nicht bestimmen oder lähmen sollte.

Die Summe unserer Erinnerungen konstituiert unser Verständnis von der Welt. Sie verleihen uns die Fähigkeit, mit Zeit und Raum in Beziehung zu treten. Gebäude und Landschaften dokumentieren das Vergangene auf andere Weisen – mitunter in greifbaren Bestandteilen oder sichtbaren Spuren von körperlicher und natürlicher Aktivität; mitunter in von Generation zu Generation überlieferten Erzählungen. Die Erinnerungen wachsen, sammeln sich an und werden in den Schichten der gebauten Substanz bewahrt. Monumente und Relikte prägen unsere kollektive Identität und helfen dabei, uns die entscheidenden Augenblicke unserer Geschichte wachzurufen. Dieser Prozess ist jedoch alles andere als statisch. Die Vergangenheit steht in einer wechselseitigen Beziehung zur Gegenwart. Die Bedeutungen, die wir unseren Bauten beifügen, sind dazu da, die Vergangenheit, die Gegenwart und die Zukunft zu definieren. Das Bewahren und Verstehen des physischen „Beweismaterials" der Vergangenheit – gleichgültig, wie unbequem sie auch sein möge – ist Teil einer gesellschaftlichen Entwicklung hin zu einer besseren Zukunft. Indem wir die Vergangenheit neben der Gegenwart in Koexistenz leben lassen, akzeptieren wir, dass unsere Gegenwart in der Zeit, die Werte und die Inhalte unserer Gesellschaft von unseren heutigen Handlungen abhängen.

Die Saalecker Werkstätten sind kein statischer Ort. Die Gebäude haben sich seit ihrer Errichtung zu Beginn des 20. Jahrhunderts mehrfach gewandelt. Im Jahr 1904 als Gemeinwesen für reformorientierte Architekt*innen und Künstler*innen gegründet, stehen sie nun im Schatten der politischen Radikalisierung von Paul Schultze-Naumburg. Der architektonische Ausdruck des ersten Gebäudes des Komplexes der Saalecker Werkstätten weist eindeutige Bezüge zur Wiener Secession, dem Wiener Werkbund und dem Deutschen Werkbund auf und spiegelt so ästhetische Ideen, wie sie zur selben Zeit auch an anderen Orten in Europa vorzufinden waren. Es weist nicht auf das verstörende Gedankengut oder das bevorstehende Grauen hin.

Unser Ansatz bei der Transformation der Saalecker Werkstätten besteht darin, die Lesbarkeit der Zeit zu vertiefen, sodass die Bauten aus einer Vielzahl von Perspektiven verstanden werden können und eben nicht nur aus der dunklen Periode der Nazi-Herrschaft. Obschon nur wenig Dokumentationsmaterial zur Geschichte der Gebäude während der vergangenen sechzig Jahre existiert, so sind die Spuren auch dieses Zeitraums von großer Bedeutsamkeit bei der Ausbildung eines adäquaten Verständnisses der Gebäudesubstanz wie der hiesigen Gemeinschaft. Während einige Teile der bestehenden Gebäude sorgsam restauriert werden, bleiben andere unberührt und fördern auf diese Weise den unterschiedlichen Gehalt zutage, der nach dem Wegzug der Familie Schultze-Naumburg gestaltet wurde. Durch eine Reihe von minimalen und dennoch wirkmächtigen Interventionen entsteht so eine neue Schicht, die dem Ort neue Werte und Inhalte verleihen.

Hier und da stellen wir historische Kennzeichen wieder her, die für das zukünftige räumliche Erleben und das Wohlbefinden der Bewohner*innen wichtig sind. Dazu zählt etwa, dass wir alte Fensteröffnungen wieder freilegen, um mehr Tageslicht in das Gebäude zu lassen und eine hellere Atmosphäre zu schaffen. Farbe dient hier als didaktisches Mittel, um eine konkrete Lesbarkeit der Zeit durch eine schichtenweise Komposition anstelle einer einfarbigen Oberfläche zu schaffen. Einige Farben werden gemäß der Farbarchäologie restauriert, während andere unberührt bleiben. Eine dritte Schicht kommt durch neue Farben aus einer Palette hinzu, die sich auf die damals in Europa herrschenden Designvorstellungen bezieht, um einen Eindruck dessen zu vermitteln, was gewesen sein könnte. Leuchtkräftige Rot- und Gelbtöne kennzeichnen die wenigen Orte, an denen erhebliche Veränderungen an der Baustruktur vorgenommen wurden.

Das Einfügen neuer Inhalte und Bedeutungen an historisch aufgeladenen Orten, erfordert nicht nur neue Funktionalität, sondern auch eine Darstellung neuer Ideale. Wir haben daher zwei Arten von Interventionen entworfen: eine, die neuer Funktionalität Platz einräumt, und eine, die neue Ideale der Diversität sowie freies Denken verkörpert. Da sich Inhalt und Funktion mit der Zeit ändern können, werden diese Interventionen so entworfen, dass sie verschoben, abgebaut oder an anderer Stelle hinzugefügt werden können. Der Garten war ursprünglich symmetrisch entlang zweier sich kreuzender Achsen angelegt und unterstrich so eine strenge Bewegungsrichtung. Indem wir eine neue Schicht von mäandernden Pfaden hinzufügen, schaffen wir neue Wege durch die Landschaft und regen die Menschen dazu an, ihre eigenen Routen zu finden, aber auch neue Nutzungsweisen für den Garten zu entdecken. In der östlichen Ecke des Gartens unterbricht eine weitere Neuigkeit – die Infinity Bridge, eine Unendlichkeitsbrücke – die alte Achse: eine symbolische Geste, die multiple Routen anstelle eines linearen Pfads schafft.

Mit dieser Brücke zwischen Vergangenheit und Gegenwart, die auf einer verschachtelten Komposition von Schichten ruht, werden die Saalecker Werkstätten gleichzeitig zu einem Ort der Reflexion und der Bildung. Die Idee der Schichtung ist keineswegs neu. Es ist die Art und Weise, wie historische Bauten und Landschaften sich allmählich in das verwandelt haben, was wir heute sehen: mit einer großen Vielfalt an Typologien, Maßstäben und Funktionen. Indem wir historischen Gebäuden erlauben, neue Funktionen, neue Werte und neue Inhalte zu beherbergen, lassen wir die Geschichte atmen und sich entwickeln, wodurch ein reicheres und vielschichtigeres Verständnis unserer Vergangenheit

und der Gegenwart entsteht. Die Transformation der Saalecker Werkstätten in einen Ort für einen Austausch über globales Design sowie eine offene und demokratische Untersuchung von Kunst und Design, ist somit eine Erinnerung daran, wie wirkmächtig Architektur sein kann.

DIEDAS – DESIGN AKADEMIE SAALECK
ORAL HISTORIES

Als Publikationspremiere der Design Akademie Saaleck bietet *Monumental Affairs_Living with Contested Spaces* eine erste Gelegenheit, das visionäre Programm und den innovativen Ansatz der jungen Institution, ihre bisherigen Leistungen und Pläne für die Zukunft im Druck zu dokumentieren.

Im Folgenden lesen Sie eine Reihe von Interviews mit den Akteur*innen und Mitwirkenden vor Ort, die die Vision der dieDAS mit Leben erfüllen. Die Gespräche wurden zwischen Januar und März 2024 geführt.

Tatjana Sprick
dieDAS Director of Program & Development (2019–)

Als Direktorin für Programm und Entwicklung ist Tatjana Sprick verantwortlich für die Planung und Durchführung der dieDAS Programme: Das reicht vom Fellowship-Programm und dem walk + talk Symposium bis hin zum Aufbau eines starken Netzwerks von Mitwirkenden, Mitarbeiter*innen und Unterstützer*innen, im Zusammenhang mit dem jeweils aktuellen Diskurs über zeitgenössische Konzepte für unsere zukünftigen Lebensräume.

Bevor sie 2019 zum Team von dieDAS stieß, war sie auf die Beratung und Betreuung von internationalen Marken und Institutionen über das gesamte kreative Spektrum hinweg bei der Entwicklung von Produkten, Kollaborationen und Visionen spezialisiert. Sie gab den Anstoß zur Design-Website L'ArcoBaleno und hat Kunden wie Fashion Council Germany, Yohji Yamamoto, Bikini Berlin, Dr. Hauschka, Elitis, The DO School sowie das Co-Retail-Geschäft ALHAMBRA BERLIN beraten.

Wann bist du zum dieDAS Team gestoßen, und was ist deine Rolle in der Organisation?

Ich hatte das Glück, dieDAS Gründungsdirektor Arne Cornelius Wasmuth 2018 kennenzulernen, also just in dem Moment, als sich gerade die Vision für die Marzona Stiftung herauszukristallisieren begann. In den entscheidenden Monaten zuvor hatte Arne entdeckt, dass die Arbeitsstätte und der historische Wohnort von Paul Schultze-Naumburg zum Verkauf standen, und so konnte schon wenig später das Objekt dank der Großzügigkeit des Sammlers und Philanthropen Egidio Marzona den Weg der Transformation beginnen. Die Marzona Stiftung wurde im Oktober 2018 von Egidio und Arne zusammen mit dem Politiker Andreas Silbersack ins Leben gerufen. Von Anfang an war mir sehr daran gelegen, mich insbesondere im Bereich der Programmleitung und der Entwicklung von Inhalten einzubringen.

Es dauerte bis zum Beginn des Jahres 2019, um die Struktur und Ziele der Stiftung zu formulieren und die erforderlichen Positionen zu umreißen. Im September desselben Jahres versammelten wir eine Gruppe anerkannter Architektur- und Designfachleute aus aller Welt, um ihnen das Grundkonzept vorzustellen: ein jährliches Residency- und Fellowship-Programm für ausgewiesene, multidisziplinäre Kreative aus den Bereichen Architektur, Design und Handwerk und ein Dokumentations- und Lernzentrum, das sich vordringlich mit der Geschichte des Standorts auseinandersetzt. Auf dieser dreitägigen Veranstaltung erörterten wir die programmatischen Ziele, das Vermächtnis des Ortes und seines Architekten sowie unsere kurz- und langfristige Vision. Mit dem Feedback der Teilnehmenden konnten wir unsere weiterführenden Pläne ausarbeiten. Wir gründeten dieDAS – Design Akademie Saaleck im Herbst 2019, und ich übernahm die Leitung der Programme und die Weiterentwicklung der dieDAS.

Warum wolltest du bei dieDAS arbeiten?

Die einmalige Gelegenheit, die Entwicklung eines Architektur- und Designlehrplans für ein Stipendienprogramm mitzuprägen, erschien mir äußerst attraktiv. Ich bin sehr dankbar, dass ich die Chance erhielt, zu den Ursprüngen des Programms beizutragen und bereits mit unserem ersten Künstlerischen Leiter, Maurizio Montalti, zusammengearbeitet zu haben. Er entwickelte die Struktur für das Programm, der wir heute noch folgen.

Wie würdest du die übergreifende Vision für dieDAS definieren?

dieDAS soll ein sogenannter freier Lernort für Designer*innen und Architekt*innen sein, die sich für den Aufbau einer egalitären, nachhaltigen, integrativen und vernetzten Zukunft verschrieben haben. Wir werfen neue Fragen rund um die menschliche Vorgehensweise im Bereich der Architektur und des Designs auf und fördern den Diskurs, immer mit einem Blick auf die Zusammenhänge, die gestern, heute und morgen miteinander verbinden. Unser Motto lautet „Gestaltung mit Haltung", was man als „Design für ein Pluriversum" übersetzen könnte.

Was sind die Schlüsselkomponenten und -ziele des Fellowship-Programms, und wie ist der Ablauf gestaltet?

Das Fellowship-Programm zielt darauf ab, die nächste Generation kreativer Führungspersönlichkeiten in den Bereichen Architektur und Design zu unterstützen, auszubilden und weiterzuentwickeln. Wir beabsichtigen, neuen Talenten einzigartige Erfahrungen, Kooperationen und Ressourcen zu bieten, damit sie die innovativen und sozial bewussten Prozesse entwickeln können, die wir dringend benötigen, um eine bessere Zukunft zu sichern.

Der Prozess beginnt bei unserer Künstlerischen Leitung. Für diese entscheidende Position suchen wir außergewöhnlich talentierte Experten, die die Grenzen ihrer Disziplinen erweitern und sozial verantwortliche Ansätze zu drängenden Fragestellungen entwickeln, wie etwa zu Nachhaltigkeit, Gleichheit und Inklusion. Während ihrer zweijährigen Wirkungszeit an der dieDAS gewähren wir unseren Künstlerischen Leiter*innen – bisher Maurizio Montalti (2020–2022) und Germane Barnes (2023–2024) – komplette kreative Freiheit bei der Ausarbeitung des Curriculums, des Fellowship-Programms und der Bestimmung des Themas des jeweiligen Jahres .

Jedes Jahr werden unsere Fellows durch ein einladungsbasiertes Auswahlverfahren ermittelt. Anhand von Empfehlungen renommierter Fachleute aus aller Welt identifizieren wir potenzielle Kandidat*innen, die hervorragende Forschung und Entwicklung in Bezug auf das Jahresthema vorzuweisen haben. Dann laden wir diese Personen ein, sich zu bewerben. Nach Eingang der Bewerbungen wählt unser wechselndes Auswahlkomitee acht Kandidat*innen aus, von denen jeder persönlich vom Künstlerischen Leiter interviewt wird, der dann vier Fellows nominiert.

Während ihres Aufenthalts auf dem dieDAS Campus durchlaufen die vier Fellows einen sorgfältig geplanten Kurs, der speziell auf ihre Bedürfnisse und das Thema der Künstlerischen Leiter*innen zugeschnitten ist. Sie erhalten kreative Orientierung, professionelle Beratung, Arbeitsräume und Unterstützung von international versierten Designer*innen und Architekt*innen, die sie entweder virtuell oder persönlich in Saaleck treffen. Zudem werden sie eingeladen, sich mit dem historischen Kontext des Ortes auseinanderzusetzen. Am Ende des Programms kuratieren die Fellows eine Ausstellung ihrer gemeinsamen Arbeiten, die bei unserem jährlichen walk + talk Symposium einem breiten internationalen Publikum präsentiert wird.

Das Curriculum zielt darauf ab, jungen Architekt*innen und Designer*innen die Möglichkeit zu geben, ihr Wissen und ihre Praxis durch das Prisma eines bestimmten Themas zu reflektieren, zu hinterfragen und hoffentlich zu erweitern. Wir bemühen uns, für sie einen Raum zu schaffen, der frei von Vorurteilen und festgefahrenen Denkweisen ist, um den Status quo zu hinterfragen und einen offenen Austausch zwischen einer ausgewählten Gruppe von internationalen Fellows und Mentor*innen zu ermöglichen. Eine entscheidende Komponente ist die Intensität der gemeinsam in einer so abgelegenen Region verbrachten Zeit, inmitten wunderschöner Natur, aber auch konfrontiert mit der unbequemen Geschichte des Ortes.

Da die historischen Gebäude auf dem Gelände noch restauriert werden müssen, ist unser gegenwärtiges Fellowship-Programm stärker eingegrenzt, als wir es uns für die Zukunft erhoffen. Nach dem Ende der Renovierungsarbeiten wird dieDAS jedes Jahr bis zu 16 internationale Fellowships mit einer Dauer von bis zu vier Monaten anbieten.

Was ist das übergreifende Ziel des walk + talk Symposiums?

Jedes Jahr im Herbst veranstaltet dieDAS zum Abschluss des Fellowship-Programms ein walk + talk Wochenende, ein transdisziplinäres Gipfeltreffen zum Jahresthema auf und um den Campus. Während dieser drei Tage sind Gäste aus dem In- und Ausland eingeladen, sich über relevante Fragen aus den Feldern Design, Handwerk und Architektur auszutauschen. Die Fellows haben die Möglichkeit, ihre Praxis und Positionen einer globalen Community vorzustellen und so einen Beitrag zum Diskurs zu leisten. Die Zusammenarbeit, die Beiträge und die Unterstützung unserer Gäste sind von unschätzbarem Wert für dieDAS und die weitere Entwicklung unserer Fellows.

Welche anderen herausragenden Leistungen sind zu erwähnen?

Ich freue mich sehr, ein paar großartige Momente aus den letzten Jahren hier hervorheben zu dürfen. Unsere erste Ausstellung zeigte Objekte aus den Jahrgängen 2020 und 2021, kuratiert von unserem Künstlerischen Leiter Maurizio Montalti. Außerdem präsentierten wir dank der kollektiven Initiative unserer Fellows des Jahres 2022 eine Ausstellung auf der Dutch Design Week im Oktober 2022.

Ein weiterer besonderer Augenblick war, als Basse Stittgen, ein Fellow unseres Debutjahrgangs, eingeladen wurde, im November 2022 an der PIN Auktion in der Pinakothek der Moderne in München teilzunehmen.

Zu guter Letzt will ich auch erwähnen, dass es eine besondere Freude war, die Podiumsdiskussion „Monumental Masterclass" zu ermöglichen, an der Student*innen unter der Künstlerischen Leitung von Germane Barnes auf der Design Miami/ 2023 teilnahmen.

Wie geht dieDas mit der lokalen Community in Sachsen-Anhalt um?

Das ist ein wichtiger Aspekt unseres Auftrags, der sich im Laufe der Zeit erweitern wird, insbesondere wenn die Renovierung der Anlage abgeschlossen ist. Bisher konnten wir Partnerschaften mit nahe gelegenen Schulen und Universitäten in Halle und Weimar durch Schülerworkshops, Aufführungen und Ausstellungen sowie durch ortsansässige Professor*innen aufbauen, die als Mentor*innen für das Fellowship-Programm und als Vortragende für die walk + talk Symposiums fungieren.

Darüber hinaus lädt dieDAS einmal im Jahr, im Frühjahr oder Frühsommer, die Öffentlichkeit ein, an unserem Tag der offenen Tür teilzunehmen und unseren Campus zu besuchen. Diese Veranstaltung, zu der jedes Jahr zwischen 300 und 400 Personen kommen, gibt uns die Gelegenheit, mit unseren Nachbarn und der breiteren regionalen Gemeinschaft in Kontakt zu treten und ihnen die Geschichte von dieDAS zu vermitteln. Die Veranstaltung trägt auch dazu bei, Kontakte zu deutschen Einrichtungen und Universitäten, wie der Burg Giebichenstein Kunsthochschule Halle und der Bauhaus-Universität Weimar zu pflegen.

Was dürfen wir in den nächsten fünf Jahren von dieDAS erwarten? Und was in den kommenden zwanzig Jahren?

Sobald der architektonische Entwurf von Dorte Mandrup umgesetzt ist – hoffentlich im Jahr 2027 –, wird die Art und Weise wachsen, wie wir den Campus und die von uns organisierten Veranstaltungen nutzen. Jedes Jahr widmen wir die Sommermonate dem Fellowship-Programm und dem walk + talk Symposiums. Die übrigen acht Monate des Jahres über wird es hier öffentliche und geschlossene Veranstaltungen geben, aber auch Workshops zusammen mit Partnerinstituten und -firmen, darunter der Harvard University Graduate School of Design. Der Standort wird über ein ständiges Café, eine Show-Küche, eine Bibliothek und Lerneinrichtungen verfügen, die nicht nur den Fellows und Gästen, sondern auch Ortsansässigen, Tourist*innen und Forschenden zugänglich sein werden.

Derzeit liegt unser Augenmerk auf der Entwicklung des dieDAS doku, unserem künftigen Dokumentationszentrum. Dieses für die Öffentlichkeit zugängliche Zentrum mit einer ausgeprägten digitalen Komponente wird Ressourcen bieten, um die Geschichte des Ortes und seines Architekten kennenzulernen und sich mit lokaler Geschichte, Genealogie sowie Rassismus- und Demokratiestudien auseinanderzusetzen. In Zusammenarbeit mit Wissenschaftler*innen und Designer*innen wird eine interaktive Medienstation vor Ort die Geschichte der Stätte und ihre Verbindung zu demokratischen Werten veranschaulichen. Darüber hinaus entwickeln wir dieDAS art, ein Programm, das zeitgenössische Kunstausstellungen an verschiedenen Orten in der Umgebung zeigt. Unser erstes Ausstellungsprojekt wurde von Daniel Marzona kuratiert, stellt die Künstler Ulla von Brandenburg und Olaf Holzapfel vor und wird am 15. Juni 2024 im Kurhaus Bad Kösen in Naumburg (Saale) eröffnet.

In den nächsten 20 Jahren hat dieDAS das Potenzial, den Campus und sein Veranstaltungsangebot noch weiter auszubauen, um noch mehr Menschen anzusprechen. Insgesamt sieht die Zukunft von dieDAS vielversprechend aus. Wir werden weiterhin in branchenführende Forschung und Entwicklung investieren und gleichzeitig sicherstellen, dass unsere Plattform antirassistische, global ausgerichtete Perspektiven fördert und einen produktiven interkulturellen und interdisziplinären Austausch zwischen verschiedenen Fellows, Fachleuten, Institutionen und Unternehmen unterstützt. Wir glauben, dass diese Bemühungen in ihrer Gesamtheit ein überzeugendes Zeugnis für die Macht des Wandels, der Gemeinschaft und der Vision darstellen.

Maurizio Montalti
Designer und erster Künstlerischer Leiter dieDAS (2020–2022)

Als erster Künstlerischer Leiter der dieDAS hat der italienische Designer Maurizio Montalti das Konzept für das dieDAS Fellowship-Programm mit erarbeitet und einen pädagogischen Rahmen geschaffen, der die Grundlage für die kommenden Jahre bilden soll. In dieser Rolle hat er die Saat gesät, aus der zukünftige Programme hervorgehen, und erste Schritte dahingehend unternommen, einen vielschichtigen Standort mit einer dunklen Vergangenheit in einen Ort für Forschung, Produktion und Diskussion zu verwandeln. Während seiner Zeit als Künstlerischer Leiter hat Montalti stets die vernetzte Natur menschlicher und nichtmenschlicher Wesen in unserem gemeinsamen Ökosystem ins Zentrum gerückt.

Neben seiner akademischen Arbeit ist Montalti Experte für Biomaterialien und ein Pionier in der Entwicklung von Pilzmyzel-basierten Technologien. Er setzt sich kritisch mit neuen und innovativen Materialien auseinander und arbeitet dabei immer im Hinblick auf die Natur. An der Schnittstelle von Design und Biotechnologie hat er das multidisziplinäre Atelier Officina Corpuscoli gegründet und ist Mitgründer von SQIM, einem Unternehmen für die Herstellung von Biomaterialien, deren Chief Mycelium Officer (Leiter Forschung und Entwicklung) er ist. SQIM vertreibt zwei Marken – mogu und ephea –, die Produkte für den täglichen Bedarf aus Biomaterialien herstellen. Sie kommen in Bereichen wie Innenarchitektur und Architektur bis hin zur Mode zum Einsatz.

Wann wurdest du Teil des dieDAS Teams? Welche Aufgabe hattest du?

Ich machte die Bekanntschaft des Teams im September 2019 während eines Symposiums das von der kurz zuvor gegründeten, aber noch nicht offiziell eröffneten dieDAS organisiert worden war. Die Anregung dazu kam unter anderem von Gründungsdirektor Arne Cornelius Wasmuth, der Leiterin Programm und Entwicklung, Tatjana Sprick, und Egidio Marzona von der Marzona Stiftung Neue Saalecker Werkstätten, Träger und Förderer der Akademie. Auf dem Event stellte die neue Akademie ihre Ziele einer kleinen Gruppe relevanter Kreativen und Pädagog*innen vor und schöpfte zugleich aus dem Erfahrungsschatz der Anwesenden. Noch war nichts formal entschieden worden, aber es gab eine starke Vision. Ich beteiligte mich rege an den verschiedenen Brainstorming-Aktivitäten und

Workshops – anscheinend so rege, dass ich hinterher eingeladen wurde, mich als Künstlerischer Leiter des Programms einzubringen. Ich nahm dieses Privileg begeistert an, und so begann das Abenteuer. Ich war der Künstlerische Leiter für das erste Fellowship-Programm im Jahr 2020 und auch in den beiden darauffolgenden Jahren, als ich die Gelegenheit hatte, in enger Synergie mit Eugenia Morpurgo als Head Mentor zu kooperieren.

Warum wolltest du mit der dieDAS zusammenarbeiten?

Mich begeisterte die Vision und die Möglichkeit, eine völlig neue Plattform zu schaffen, etwas, das anders war als die bereits existierenden Fellowships und Residency-Programme. Ich selbst hatte in der Vergangenheit andernorts bereichernde Erfahrungen als Fellow gemacht. Und ich dachte mir, es könnte interessant sein, die besten Aspekte aus all diesen Erfahrungen zu übernehmen und das Wissen zu nutzen, wie andere Programme funktionieren, während wir unser eigenes aufbauen.

Wir fingen sozusagen mit einer komplett leeren Leinwand an. Es gab viele Imponderabilien, etwa die Frage, wie sich der physische Raum, der nicht für ein Programm wie das unsere ausgelegt war, entwickeln würde. Obwohl das Vorhaben in mancher Hinsicht an dem spezifischen Ort auch furchteinflößend war, so eröffneten sich doch gerade hier eine Reihe von Möglichkeiten. Anstelle der üblichen hierarchischen, vertikalen Pyramidenstruktur etwa gab es den Wunsch, ein Programm zu schaffen, das auf Funktionen, Fähigkeiten und Kooperation basiert. So gelang es uns sogar, in der pädagogischen Struktur einige der Werte umzusetzen, auf denen dieDAS fußt – speziell die Inklusivität sowie die Fähigkeit, offene, konstruktive Dialoge zwischen den Praktizierenden unterschiedlichster Disziplinen und Hintergründe zu fördern. Die Vorstellung, bei der Schaffung einer Plattform mitzuhelfen, die einen positiven Beitrag zur Erweiterung des kritischen Diskurses leisten könnte – insbesondere zu Themen, die mir sehr am Herzen liegen, nämlich soziale und ökologische Gerechtigkeit –, war äußerst verlockend.

Die Aufgabe, dieses an einem so herausfordernden Standort zu tun, war ebenfalls faszinierend. Der Ort stellt zwar zweifellos aus vielerlei Gründen eine Herausforderung dar, ist aber dennoch interessant durch die Abgeschiedenheit, die er bietet. Auch die Geschichte der gesamten Region ist spannend, wo vor annähernd hundert Jahren die Bauhaus-Bewegung entstand. Die Vorstellung, ein Jahrhundert später zum Entstehen einer neuen Bewegung einen Beitrag leisten zu können, die Design und den kreativen Diskurs im Allgemeinen positiv beeinflussen könnte, hat mich vor allem dazu bewegt, hier mitmachen zu wollen.

Du hast einige der Schlüsselwerte der dieDAS angesprochen. Wie würdest du die übergreifende Vision und die entscheidenden Ziele des Fellowship-Programms definieren?

Ich glaube die Vision der dieDAS besteht darin, einen Raum für kreative Begegnungen zu schaffen, in dem unterschiedliche Ideen aufeinandertreffen. Um das zu erreichen, fördern wir die kreative Produktion, die durch kritische Analysen mit ausgewiesenen Fachleuten – primär aus den Bereichen Design und Architektur, dann aber auch aus dem Handwerk und darüber hinaus – unterstützt wird. Die Idee war, Menschen mit den unterschiedlichsten Hintergründen aus Kreativität, Bildung, Kultur und anderem zusammenzubringen und zu untersuchen, welche Art von Erkenntnissen dadurch entstehen würden. Außerdem genossen wir den Luxus, dies ohne die Notwendigkeit zu tun, traditionelle Leistungsindikatoren und Ähnliches festzulegen. Sowohl die Organisation als auch ich gingen an das Vorhaben als Experiment heran, ein Abenteuer, das in einem Ansatz des praxisorientierten Lernens wurzelte, dem sogenannten Learning by Doing. In dieser Hinsicht war es eine äußerst inspirierende Zeit.

Hand in Hand mit dem Aufbau des Fellowship-Programms war ein weiteres Ziel die Schaffung und Einbindung einer Community. So gelang es uns, auf das Fachwissen eines Netzwerks zurückzugreifen und gleichzeitig relevante Inhalte anzubieten, die wiederum weitere Beteiligte ermutigten sich zu engagieren. Wir fingen klein an, gingen von den persönlichen Kontakten des Teams aus, und seither ist das Ganze stetig über die Jahre gewachsen.

Apropos Fachwissen, könntest du uns etwas zur Rolle der Mentoren und Mentorinnen im Fellowship-Programm sagen, und wie sie ausgewählt werden?

Die Mentor*innen bieten den Fellows Inspiration und kritische Orientierungshilfe. Sie kommen aus vielen verschiedenen Disziplinen und Fachrichtungen und werden in der Regel eingeladen, um Fallbeispiele aus ihrer eigenen, oft außergewöhnlichen Praxis anzuführen, die mit dem jeweiligen Jahresthema in Verbindung stehen. Ein Beispiel hierfür ist David Zilber, ein Koch und Ernährungswissenschaftler, der zuvor das Noma Fermentation Lab geleitet hat. Er sprach 2022 über die Vorstellung von Stoffwechsel als Teil einer Praxis, die von Anwendungen bei

Nahrungsmitteln über wissenschaftliche Forschung bis hin zur Materialproduktion reicht. Unser Interesse ist es, mitunter unerwartete Vortragende einzuladen, die nicht nur von theoretischen Aspekten sprechen, sondern vielmehr konkrete Beispiele für die Umsetzung dieser Theorien im Alltag bieten.

Anfänge sind immer interessant. Besonders faszinierend ist es, ein Programm zu erschaffen, das sich im Erfolgsfall weit über deinen anfänglichen Beitrag hinaus entwickelt und ausdehnt. Wie bist du es angegangen, die Ziele der Akademie zum Leben zu erwecken und zugleich die Grundlage für weitere dieDAS Themen und zukünftige Kooperationen zu schaffen?

Ja, in dieser Hinsicht war es entscheidend, ein Umfeld zu schaffen, das auf wechselseitigem Respekt aufbaut, einen Raum, in dem jede Stimme gleiches Gewicht hat und in dem ein ebenso kritischer wie konstruktiver Dialog gedeihen kann. Unser Learning-by-Doing-Ansatz zielte darauf ab, jeder späteren Künstlerischen Leitung zu ermöglichen, ein relevantes Thema zu identifizieren, das sich dann von den Fellows, Praktiker*innen und Vortragenden aus unterschiedlichsten Disziplinen von zahlreichen Standpunkten aus analysieren lässt. Als Künstlerischer Leiter war es mir auch wichtig, offene Rahmenbedingungen zu schaffen und unsere Teilnehmerinnen und Teilnehmer zu ermutigen, im Laufe unseres zweiwöchigen, superintensiven Programms jene Rahmenbedingungen selbst mitzugestalten. So wurde auch den Fellows ein Teil der Verantwortung für das Programm übertragen, und wir lernten alle gemeinsam.

Die Strategie, die sich herauskristallisiert hat, lag darin, kreative Praktiken als Katalysatoren für die Analyse von Fragen unserer Zeit zu nutzen. Wir verwendeten kreatives und kritisches Denken sowie all die Werkzeuge, die damit assoziiert werden, um Umweltfragen und Problemstellungen der sozialen Gerechtigkeit zu betrachten – all dies verwurzelt in unserer Beziehung zur Materialität und dem Ökosystem des Standorts. Wir waren überzeugt davon, dass dieser Weg sich mit der Zeit ausgezeichnet entwickeln würde.

Ich wünschte, wir hätten mehr Mittel gehabt, unsere Arbeit von Anfang an aufzuzeichnen. Das war eines der Ziele, die wir verfehlt haben. Ich denke, es ist wichtig, unsere pädagogischen und kooperativen Anstrengungen zu dokumentieren, insbesondere hinsichtlich der so aktuellen Themen – zum Nutzen früherer und zukünftiger Teilnehmer*innen, aber auch für die globale Community. Ich bin dankbar, dass diese Publikation dazu beitragen kann,

einige dieser Anstrengungen zu kommunizieren, und hoffe, dass zukünftige Programme ähnlich gut dokumentiert werden.

Angesichts deines professionellen Fokus auf innovative Biomaterialien, regeneratives Design und symbiotische Beziehungen zwischen Menschen und nichtmenschlichen Wesen ist es auch bemerkenswert, dass dein Ansatz für das dieDAS Programm – ebenso wie die von dir gewählten Themen – ein auf gegenseitigen Respekt und Achtung basierendes Umfeld in den Mittelpunkt stellt. Stets ermutigst du zu Achtsamkeit und hast so ein wirklich besonderes Umfeld geschaffen. Kannst du diesen Ansatz erläutern?

Du hast es perfekt formuliert. Mein Wunsch war es von Anfang an, ein Programm zu entwickeln, das nicht nur in der Theorie, sondern vor allem in der Praxis und im Handeln verwurzelt ist. Im ersten Jahr des Fellowship-Programms lautete unser Thema *Farming Materials' Ecologies: From Uncomfortable Pasts to Responsible Futures*. Wir arbeiteten in einem äußerst minimalistischen Umfeld – zu der Zeit hatten die Renovierungsarbeiten noch nicht begonnen und waren noch nicht einmal abschließend geplant worden. Für uns war genau das die Gelegenheit, etwas Neues zu schaffen, nicht nur metaphorisch, sondern auch praktisch. So haben wir darüber nachgedacht, wie wichtig es ist, ein erneuertes Ökosystem an einem Standort zu schaffen, dessen Wurzeln in einem so finsteren Kapitel der Geschichte stecken. Wir wollten zeigen, dass es möglich ist, in eine verantwortungsvolle Zukunft aufzubrechen, wenn man bei diesen Wurzeln, buchstäblich vom Boden ausgehend beginnt. Dementsprechend begannen wir ein Ökosystem aus unterschiedlichen Organismen zu pflanzen, die sich gegenseitig stützen – in unmittelbarem Gegensatz zum repressiven Geist des Nationalsozialismus. Wir sahen eine Gelegenheit, kollaborativ zwischen den Disziplinen zu agieren, um so die Basis zu legen für ein vollständig integriertes Ökosystem, in dem jedes handelnde Wesen in Synergie mit den anderen arbeitet. Dieser Ansatz hat sich kontinuierlich weiterentwickelt und ist über die folgenden zwei Jahre gewachsen: mit den Titeln *Symbiotic Habitat: Growing Regenerative Connections* im Jahr 2021 und *Designing Metabolic Relations – How Can We Build Regenerative Systems?* im Jahr 2022.

Obwohl jedes der drei von mir kuratierten Fellowship-Programme eigene Nuancen und eine Vielzahl an unterschiedlichen Partner*innen hatte, bildeten sie kumulativ den Versuch, unterschiedliche Perspektiven einzubeziehen, um Wege zu finden, unsere gestörte Beziehung zur Umwelt neu zu definieren. Und das nicht nur theoretisch, sondern auf eine handfeste, immersive Weise.

Ich bin davon überzeugt, dass diese Arbeit ein solides Fundament für die Zukunft gelegt hat. Es war daher besonders inspirierend für mich zu beobachten, wie Germane Barnes' Programm sich mit dem Standort auseinandergesetzt und das dieDAS Programm nachhaltig geprägt hat. Ich freue mich auf alle kommenden Jahrgänge.

Eugenia Morpurgo
dieDAS Head Mentor (2021–2022)

Die in Venedig lebende Designerin Eugenia Morpurgo arbeitete mit dieDAS an den ersten drei Fellowship-Programmen zusammen. Sie beeindruckte den Künstlerischen Leiter Maurizio Montalti 2020 in ihrer Rolle als Mentorin eines Ein-Tages-Workshops so sehr, dass er sie einlud, Head Mentor zu werden und 2021 und 2022 eng mit ihm an der Entwicklung des Lehrplans sowie dessen Umsetzung zu arbeiten.

Morpurgo studierte Social Design an der Design Academy Eindhoven (MA, 2011) und Industriedesign an der Università Iuav di Venezia (BA, 2009). Ihre forschungsorientierte Praxis untersucht das Potenzial der Agrarökologie bei der Schaffung regenerativer Produktionsprozesse für Naturstoffe, Färbemittel und Klebstoffe in Bezug auf Artenvielfalt und die Abhängigkeit von Jahreszeiten. Ihre Arbeit wurde ausgestellt unter anderem im MAXXI – Museo nazionale delle arti del XXI secolo in Rom, in der Triennale Milano, im Total Museum of Contemporary Art in Seoul, im New Yorker Textile Arts Center sowie im Z33 – Haus für zeitgenössische Kunst in Hasselt. Zusammen mit Olivia de Gouveia hat sie The Future Continuous gegründet.

Wann bist du zum dieDAS Team gestoßen und wie lange warst du dabei?

Meine Zusammenarbeit mit der dieDAS begann mit dem ersten Fellowship-Programm im Jahr 2020. Der Künstlerische Leiter Maurizio Montalti bat mich zunächst, Mentorin für einen Ein-Tages-Workshop zu sein. Danach lud er mich ein, eine größere Rolle zu übernehmen und zusammen mit ihm an der Kuratierung der folgenden beiden Fellowship-Programm 2021 und 2022 zu arbeiten.

Wie würdest du die Vision für dieDAS definieren und was hat dich dazu bewogen, ein Teil davon zu werden?

Meiner Meinung nach existiert die Vision der dieDAS auf mehreren Ebenen gleichzeitig. Die Akademie hat das Ziel, ein Zentrum kritischer zeitgenössischer Kultur für die Kreativindustrie zu werden. Als solches stellt sie sich der Geschichte des Ortes und erkennt die politische Dimension von Kultur klar an. Unabhängig davon bringt die jeweilige Künstlerische Leitung ihre eigene Vision in das alljährliche Fellowship-Programm mit ein. Das verengt den Fokus, je nach den konkreten Interessens- bzw. Forschungsgebieten des Künstlerischen Direktors.

In meiner Zusammenarbeit mit Maurizio konzentrierte sich die Vision darauf, tief in die ökologische Nachhaltigkeit von Baustoffen einzutauchen, insbesondere in Bezug auf ihre Verwendung im Design – von der Mode bis hin zur Architektur. Dabei arbeiteten wir mit den Fellows und einer Reihe von internationalen Experten zusammen. Dieses spezifische Thema und das auf Austausch und Dialog aufgebaute Format der Fellowships haben mich überzeugt, ein Teil der dieDAS sein zu wollen.

Wie würdest du die entscheidenden Ziele des dieDAS Fellowship-Programms definieren? Und wie ermöglichen die Mentorinnen und Mentoren das Erreichen dieser Ziele?

Eines der wesentlichen Ziele besteht darin, die Grenzen der Disziplin zu sprengen. Die Fellows haben zusammen mit der Künstlerischen Leitung die Gelegenheit zuzuhören und in Dialog mit Fachleuten aus aller Welt und aus der Region zu treten. Die internationalen Mentorinnen und Mentoren teilen ihre kritischen und topaktuellen Erkenntnisse aus den jeweiligen Fachbereichen, während die regionalen die Fellows dabei unterstützen, ihre Überlegungen im ökologischen und historischen Kontext zu erden. Durch die gemeinsam verbrachte Zeit und die dabei aufkommenden Fragen und Diskussionen wachsen alle Beteiligten – ebenso wie die Disziplinen Design und Architektur.

Wie würdest du deine Rolle als Head Mentor beschreiben?

Maurizio und ich haben uns bei der Kuratierung des Fellowship-Programms dank unserer ähnlichen Forschungsansätze ergänzt, vor allem in Bezug auf Material. Meine Forschung konzentriert sich auf agrarökologische Landbaupraktiken für die Produktion von Materialien. Maurizio arbeitet hingegen mit Biofabrikation. Durch die Verbindung unserer jeweiligen Perspektiven konnten wir das Thema der ökologischen Nachhaltigkeit von Baustoffen kritischer betrachten. Das wiederum regte die Fellows und auch uns dazu an, noch intensiver über die Zukunft von Materialien und die sozioökonomischen Systeme, die sie produzieren, nachzudenken.

Sowohl die Beiträge der Mentorinnen und Mentoren als auch die Erkenntnisse aus den kritischen Diskussionen zwischen den Fellows, Maurizio und mir haben mich bereichert, beruflich wie auch persönlich.

Wie hat sich das Fellowship-Programm aus der Sicht des Head Mentor während der ersten Jahre entwickelt?

Eine wichtige Lernerfahrung im ersten Jahr des Fellowship-Programms, die sich stark auf die Organisation des zweiten Jahres auswirkte, war die Zeit an sich. Uns wurde klar, dass es während

der zwei Wochen wichtiger ist, Raum für Dialog und Nachdenken zu lassen, als jede Minute des Programms mit Aktivitäten auszufüllen. Die Zeit zum Nachdenken erlaubte uns allen, die bereichernden Impulse aus den Vorträgen und Ausflügen erst angemessen zu verarbeiten.

Die Ergebnisse des zweiten Fellowships haben uns wiederum gezeigt, dass es in den kurzen zwei Wochen entscheidend ist, die Fellows zu motivieren, miteinander zu kooperieren. 2021 arbeiteten die Fellows zusammen am Bau einer kleinen Myzelien-Architektur. Durch die Arbeit auf ein gemeinsames Ziel hin haben sie sich auch kritische Fragen über ihre eigene Praxis gestellt. Im Jahr 2022 dann, als sie etwas individuell produzieren sollten, verfielen die Fellows in ihre gewohnten Arbeitsweisen.

Kannst du bitte einige Höhepunkte der Fellowship-Programme mit uns teilen, die du begleitet hast?

Im Fellowship 2021 war der Prozess, eine kleine Struktur aus Weide und Myzelium zu bauen, eine großartige Erfahrung. Der Weg vom ersten Zuhören über das Fragen nach unserer Beziehung zu nichtmenschlichen Wesen bis hin zum Arbeiten mit lebendigem Myzelium, aus dem eine Behausung für Menschen werden sollte – all das löste intensive Gespräche aus. Diese Erfahrung hat meines Erachtens alle berührt, die daran beteiligt waren.

Während des Fellowship 2022 verbrachten wir einen Tag damit, die Umgebung des dieDAS Campus nach Nahrung, Heilmitteln, Materialien und Färbemitteln abzusuchen. Das ließ uns über den Wert nachdenken, den wir den Arten beimessen, die uns mit diesen lebenswichtigen Ressourcen versorgen. Dies unterbrach die distanzierten Beziehungen, die durch traditionelle Produktions- und Konsumprozesse zwischen den Verbrauchern und Verbraucherinnen sowie der Herkunft der von uns genutzten Ressourcen entstehen.

Wo siehst du den konkreten Beitrag des dieDAS Fellowship-Programms zur internationalen Designkultur?

Für die teilnehmenden Personen ist es meines Erachtens großartig, eine so intensive Erfahrung zu machen, die ihre Praxis bereichern wird – und hoffentlich in Zukunft auch die ganze internationale Designkultur.

Durch eine gezieltere Dokumentation der ersten Fellowship-Programme, einschließlich der Beiträge der Mentorinnen und Mentoren sowie der Ideen der Fellows, hätten die Prozesse und Ergebnisse noch umfangreicher geteilt und zu einem bedeutsamen Referenzpunkt für die internationale Designkultur werden können.

163

Was erhoffst du dir für die zukünftige Entwicklung des Programms?

Ich hoffe das Programm findet seine Akzeptanz in der Community vor Ort und schafft eine Brücke zu schlagen zwischen zeitlich begrenzten Erfahrungen – wie denen der Fellowships – und dem Ziel einer lang anhaltenden Wirkung.

Zeno Franchini
dieDAS Head Mentor (2023–2024) und Fellow (2021)

Der in Palermo lebende Social Designer Zeno Franchini ist gegenwärtig Head Mentor des die-DAS Fellowship-Programms auf Einladung des Künstlerischen Leiters Germane Barnes. In dessen zweijährigem Engagement wurden anhand der Inhalte des Fellowship-Programms Fragen der sozialen, aber auch der ökologischen Gerechtigkeit erforscht, und zwar über die Themen *Monumental Affairs* (2023) und *Material Evidence* (2024). Im Jahr 2021 hatte Franchini selbst als Fellow am dieDAS Fellowship-Programm teilgenommen.

Nach seinem Master-Abschluss in Social Design an der Design Academy Eindhoven gründete Franchini zusammen mit der Designerin Francesca Gattello 2014 Marginal Studio. Das Duo produziert Prototypen, Installationen, Texte und Filme, die sich mit dem Klimawandel, der Dekolonialisierung und dem politischen Wandel auseinandersetzen. Ihr Schwerpunkt liegt auf marginalisierten Gemeinschaften, vernachlässigten Umweltbereichen und Zonen an der gesellschaftlichen Peripherie. Die Arbeit von Marginal Studio wurde unter anderem auf der 58. Biennale von Venedig, der Manifesta 12 sowie im Triennale-Museum in Mailand gezeigt.

Wann bist du zum dieDAS Team gestoßen und wie lange warst du dabei?

Ich wurde zunächst 2021 eingeladen, eine Bewerbung für ein Fellowship einzureichen. Als Social Designer in Palermo war ich äußerst fasziniert von der Offenheit und dem Engagement für die Forschung, die Maurizio Montalti und Eugenia Morpurgo durch ihren Aufruf für Fellows vermittelten. Ich kannte ihre Arbeit und war dementsprechend neugierig auf den Aufenthalt. In der Designwelt ist es äußerst selten, auf aufrichtiges Interesse an Forschung und sozialem Engagement zu stoßen.

Für mich war das dieDAS Fellowship ein ganz besonderes Erlebnis, in dessen Nachklang ich mich weiter für das Programm, seine Aktivitäten und Entwicklungen interessierte. Zwei Jahre später kam ich zu meiner Überraschung in die engere Auswahl für die Stelle des Head Mentor für das 2023er-Fellowship unter dem Künstlerischen Leiter Germane Barnes. Ich denke, dass ich mit meiner Sicht von außen einerseits und meiner Kenntnis des Fellowship Programms von innen auf der anderen Seite, einen Beitrag leisten konnte – durch meine eigenen Erfahrungen als Teilnehmer an dem Programm ebenso wie durch meine Vertrautheit mit dem Thema, das Germane für 2023 vorgegeben hatte, nämlich *Monumental Affairs*.

Wie würdest du die übergreifende Idee der dieDAS definieren, und was hat dich dazu bewogen, Teil der Akademie sein zu wollen?

Der offene Geist des Fellowship-Programms macht die Arbeit fruchtbar und im Wesentlichen ergebnisoffen. Allerdings fordert der Ort mit seinem schwierigen Erbe im unmittelbaren Kontext der Architektur eine intensive Auseinandersetzung. Diese Polaritäten helfen dabei, mit der Vielfalt des Inputs im Programm umzugehen. Auch wenn die Beiträge der Teilnehmer und Teilnehmerinnen divers sind, so sind doch die Fragen, die in der Luft liegen, sehr klar und eindeutig. Die schrecklichen Ereignisse unserer Vergangenheit zu verstehen, führt unmittelbar dazu, eine Zukunft in den Blick zu nehmen, in der diese Fehler nicht wiederholt werden.

Wie würdest du die wesentlichen Ziele des die-DAS Fellowship-Programms formulieren, und wie helfen Mentoren und Mentorinnen beim Erreichen dieser Ziele?

Das Programm erlaubt es den Fellows, ihren eigenen Weg zu finden – gesellschaftliche Fragen aus ihrer eigenen Perspektive heraus anzugehen. Auf kuratorischer Ebene ändert sich der thematische Schwerpunkt von Jahr zu Jahr, doch bleibt eine grundlegende Haltung, die danach strebt zu verstehen, wie wir gemeinsam auf demselben Planeten in einer gerechteren und kollektiv organisierten Gesellschaft zusammenleben können. Alle Teilnehmer und Teilnehmerinnen bringen ihre eigenen Positionierungen in das jeweilige Thema ein.

Wie würdest du deine Rolle als Head Mentor charakterisieren?

Als Head Mentor koordiniere ich und wähle die anderen Mentoren des Fellowship-Programms sowie die Aktivitäten für die Fellows aus. Ich fungiere als Vermittler der Vision der Künstlerischen Leitung und arbeite im Dialog mit den Mentoren und Fellows. Ich betrachte das Fellowship als eine Erfahrung, die aus einer Reihe von Augenblicken besteht. Diese umfassen weit mehr als nur die Vorträge der Mentoren. Vielmehr schließen sie sämtliche gemeinsame Erlebnisse ein, von Spaziergängen über Mahlzeiten hin zu Gesprächen und vielem mehr. Diese Momente tragen zu einem dynamischen Austausch unter den Fellows bei, aber auch zu ihrem Gefühl für den Ort.

Wie hat sich deine Arbeit als Head Mentor auf deine eigene Praxis ausgewirkt?

Meine Erfahrung als Head Mentor hat mein Verständnis für das Thema Rassismus im Design erweitert. Das Thema ist Teil meiner täglichen Praxis im Umgang mit Migranten-Communities in Palermo. Meine Arbeit konzentriert sich auf das kollektive Schaffen und die kollektive materielle Kultur als Mittel, um Geschichten zu erzählen und Gemeinsamkeiten zu finden.

Meine Zusammenarbeit mit Germane im Rahmen des dieDAS Programms bot mir die Gelegenheit, aus meinen privaten wie beruflichen Erfahrungen heraus Inhalte beizutragen, speziell über die afroamerikanische Perspektive, aber auch die theoretische und akademische Sicht auf den Rassismus im Allgemeinen zu entdecken. Das alles vor dem Hintergrund des rassistischen Erbes von Paul Schultze-Naumburg und des Nazi-Regimes.

Wie würdest du den einzigartigen Beitrag des Fellowship-Programms zur internationalen Design-Kultur beschreiben?

Im Spektrum des europäischen Designs bleiben die schmerzhaften und schwierigeren Themen häufig ausgespart. Stattdessen wird eine unproblematische Positivität in den Mittelpunkt gerückt – was gewiss einfacher, wenn auch weniger relevant ist. Mit Reflexionen über Themen wie Rassismus und gesellschaftliche Exklusion können wir jedoch einen echten Beitrag zum kulturellen Diskurs leisten, aus dem die Gesellschaft auch jenseits von Design und Architektur Nutzen ziehen kann. Selbst in der kurzen Dauer eines dieDAS Fellowships lassen sich Richtungen andeuten, auf die wir kollektiv hinarbeiten können, mehr noch als konkrete Lösungen aufzeigen.

In dieser Oase der Designforschung, die in die Landschaft wie in die überregionale Geschichte eingebunden ist, arbeite ich auf eine Zukunft hin, in der Kollegen und Kolleginnen diesen Ort als ein Prisma betrachten werden, durch das sie die Welt in all ihren Ungerechtigkeiten und Konflikten kritisch verstehen können.

Meine Hoffnung ist, dass gerade an diesem Ort, an dem einst Unterdrückung und Ausgrenzung artikuliert worden sind – eine Weltanschauung, die sich nicht wesentlich von heutigen extremistischen Ideologien unterscheidet –, Designer*innen und Architekt*innen in die Lage versetzt werden, ihre eigene Rolle beim Abbau gefährlicher Strukturen erkennen zu können, indem sie die Verflechtungen zwischen allen Menschen und Dingen zu würdigen lernen.

Basse Stittgen
dieDAS Fellow (2020) und Mitglied des
Auswahlkomitees (2022)

Der in Hannover geborene und jetzt in Amsterdam lebende Basse Stittgen war 2020 Fellow im ersten Jahr des dieDAS Fellowship-Programms unter der Künstlerischen Leitung von Maurizio Montalti. Zwei Jahre später wurde er eingeladen als Jurymitglied dabei mitzuwirken, die Fellows für das Jahr 2022 auszuwählen.

An der Schnittstelle von Design, Kunst und Materialforschung zielt Stittgens Praxis darauf ab, Objekten auf immer neue Weisen ihr Potenzial, zeitgenössische Komplexitäten zu vermitteln, zu entlocken. Seit seinem Abschluss an der Design Akademie Eindhoven 2017 sind Arbeiten von ihm im Victoria and Albert Museum, im Stedelijk Museum Amsterdam, der National Gallery of Victoria in Melbourne sowie auf der 13. Shanghai Architektur-Biennale ausgestellt worden. Seine Werke finden sich unter anderem auch in den ständigen Sammlungen des MAK Wien sowie des Museum de Fundatie in Zwolle.

Wie würdest du die übergreifende Vision der die-DAS und ihres Fellowship-Programms definieren? Und warum wolltest du ein Teil davon sein?

Meiner Erfahrung nach möchte dieDAS Verbindungen herstellen. Als Ort ist die Akademie zugleich kritisch und optimistisch. Sie funktioniert auf zahlreichen Ebenen: zwischen Mensch und Land, Mensch und Geschichte, aber auch zwischen den teilnehmenden Fellows selbst.

Ich habe mich aus einer Reihe von Gründen beworben, vor allem aber weil ich lernen und Kontakte knüpfen möchte. Die Saalecker Werkstätten und die historisch teilweise von dort ausgehende hasserfüllte Ideologie sind eine Belastung. Das Programm der dieDAS bot mir in diesem Kontext die Möglichkeit, mich sowohl mit meiner Rolle als Künstler als auch als Deutscher auseinanderzusetzen. Es gab uns allen – den internationalen Fellows, Mentor*innen und anderen Mitarbeiter*innen – die Chance, ein neues Narrativ für diesen Ort zu entwerfen und aktiv mitzugestalten.

Wie lief der Bewerbungsprozess bei dir ab? Was wolltest du unbedingt kommunizieren?

Ich erinnere mich an eine Frage während des Bewerbungsverfahrens, die sich auf die Politik in meiner Arbeit bezog. Obwohl ich mich selbst nicht als politische Person sehe und meine Arbeit nicht bewusst politisch ist, betrachte ich mich durchaus als sozial und meine Arbeit als sozial engagiert. Durch diesen Ansatz schließt meine Arbeit das Politische mit ein, indem sie eine klare Position bezieht und Aufmerksamkeit auf das Verborgene und Übersehene lenkt.

Welche Auswirkungen des Fellowships auf deine Praxis hast du erwartet?

Da meine Praxis sich um Materialität dreht, betrachtete ich das Stipendium als eine Möglichkeit, mein Verständnis für die Verflechtungen zwischen Materie, Ort und Zeit zu vertiefen und durch diese Perspektive meine Kenntnisse der materiellen Kultur zu verfeinern. Die von dieDAS eingeladenen Experten und Expertinnen inspirierten mich dazu, mit neuen Design-Methoden zu experimentieren und den Horizont meiner Arbeit zu erweitern. So konnte ich neue soziomaterielle Interaktionen kritisch untersuchen und Wege finden, mich in Bezug auf die aktuellen, höchst dringlichen Fragestellungen im Design zu positionieren.

Bitte nenne doch eine paar Höhepunkte aus deiner Zeit als Fellow.

Das erste Fellowship fand während der Pandemie statt, und anfangs gab es viele Unsicherheiten, ob es überhaupt durchgeführt werden kann. Ein erster Höhepunkt war also, dass wir alle überhaupt nach Saaleck kommen und diesen Ort gemeinsam nutzen konnten. Da die Pandemie unsere Arbeitsmöglichkeiten einschränkte, nutzten wir die Chance, gemeinsam über zukünftige Szenarien für die Saalecker Werkstätten nachzudenken und unsere eigene Praxis zu reflektieren. Der ergebnisoffene Prozess, der durch das reichhaltige, von dieDAS organisierte Vortragsprogramm gefördert wurde, ist das, was mir besonders in Erinnerung bleibt.

Was ist dir von deiner Erfahrung als Fellow geblieben?

Vor allem die familiäre Atmosphäre mit allen Beteiligten ist für mich prägend gewesen. Ich fühle mich als Teil einer im Wachsen begriffenen Community.

Wie hast du deine Erfahrung als Fellow in deiner späteren Arbeit für das Auswahlkomitee angewendet?

Für mich persönlich ist das Material ein Prisma für das Soziale. Daher achtete ich beim Durchsehen der Bewerbungen besonders auf Projekte, die diese Verknüpfungen in sinnvoller Weise herstellen konnten. Ich bin überzeugt, dass diese Sichtweise unumgänglich ist, um sich mit der Örtlichkeit, der Historie und der Zukunft der Saalecker Werkstätten auseinanderzusetzen.

Wie war deine Zusammenarbeit mit den anderen Komiteemitgliedern?

Für mich als relativ jungen und unerfahrenen Designer war es schon eine aufregende Sache, Teil eines so ehrwürdigen Komitees zu sein. Mir fiel jedoch bald auf, dass alle einander ausreden ließen. Wir führten äußerst stimulierende Gespräche, da die Qualität der Bewerbungen ausgezeichnet war.

Welche Erwartungen hast du an die zukünftige Entwicklung des Programms?

Ich sehe dieDAS als einen Ort, der die internationale Design-Community dazu inspirieren kann, ihre Gewohnheiten, Entwicklungen und Beziehungen zu materiellen Objekten zu überdenken. Sie ist ein Ort, an dem wir uns mit der eigentlichen Aufgabe von Design auseinandersetzen können – zu heilen, statt Schaden zuzufügen.

Sasson Rafailov
dieDAS Fellow (2020) und Mitglied des Auswahlkomitees (2023)

Der in Virginia lebende Designer, Handwerker und Hochschullehrer Sasson Rafailov war 2020 Fellow im ersten dieDAS Fellowship-Programm unter der Künstlerischen Leitung von Maurizio Montalti. Zwei Jahre später saß er in der Jury für die Auswahl zur Teilnahme am Fellowship-Programm des Jahres 2023.

Sein Bachelor-Studium schloss Sasson 2018 an der Cornell University ab, wo er sich mit Design-Pädagogik beschäftigt hatte. Danach unterrichtete er einen Kurs zu Grundlagentheorien an der School of Architecture and Planning der University at Buffalo. Anschließend absolvierte er das Master-of-Design-Programm an der Harvard Graduate School of Design (GSD), das er 2021 abschloss. Zurzeit arbeitet er an einem PhD in Constructed Environment an der University of Virginia School of Architecture. In seiner Dissertation schlägt er vom Standpunkt einer posthumanistischen Philosophie aus einen neuen Ansatz zum Handwerk in der Ausbildung von Architektinnen und Architekten vor. Das Projekt nutzt Begriffe aus der neuen materialistischen Literatur, wie zum Beispiel „agentieller Realismus", „materielle Intelligenz", „nichthierarchische Ontologien" und „Verkörperung". So entsteht eine Sicht auf Handwerksproduktion, die Menschen erlaubt, auf ethischere und nachhaltigere Weise mit der materiellen Welt zu interagieren.

Wie würdest du die Vision der dieDAS und ihres Fellowship-Programms beschreiben? Und warum wolltest du dich daran beteiligen?

dieDAS ist ein Ort des Experimentierens. Im weitesten Sinne verstehe ich dieDAS als ein Angebot, Beziehungen zwischen Designer*innen zu ihren Communities neu zu denken. dieDAS ermöglicht eine neue Herangehensweise an zwischenmenschliche Netzwerke, bis hin zur Frage, wie Designer*innen ihre Rolle unter den Organismen und Materialien verstehen, die ihr Leben und ihre Praktiken bestimmen.

Diese innovative Sichtweise wird in erster Linie dadurch ermöglicht, dass junge Künstler*innen, Designer*innen und Kunsthandwerker*innen neue Arbeitsweisen kennenlernen, die ihre vorgefassten Meinungen infrage stellen. Sie werden dazu ermutigt, produktive neue Verbindungen zu anderen Fellows, zu Mitgliedern der lokalen Communities und zu nichtmenschlichen Wesen in der Landschaft aufzubauen.

Ich war begeistert, ein Teil des ersten Fellowships zu sein, weil ich zu dieser Zeit in meiner praktischen Arbeit nach neuen Wegen gesucht habe, mit Materialien umzugehen. Ich begann ein Verhältnis zu Stein, Holz und Ton zu entwickeln, das über das rein Nutzenbasierte und Instrumentelle hinausgeht, aber ich war mir noch nicht sicher, wie ich diese neuen Richtungen weiter erkunden konnte.

Das Thema des ersten Fellowships, „Landwirtschaftliche Materialökologie – aus einer unbequemen Vergangenheit in eine verantwortungsbewusste Zukunft" versprach meinen Horizont hinsichtlich der Rolle von Materialien zu erweitern. Ebenso wollte ich mit anderen Designschaffenden in Kontakt kommen, die meine Überlegungen beeinflussen könnten.

Wie gestaltete sich der Bewerbungsprozess?

In der Bewerbung wurde deutlich mehr gefordert, als ich dies von anderen Summer-Fellowships kannte. So war ich gezwungen, über Erfahrungen nachzudenken, die ich ansonsten noch nicht so stark reflektiert hatte, obwohl sie für meinen Designansatz durchaus prägend waren. Mir fiel auf, dass sich die Fragen trotz eines unterschiedlichen Wortlauts in erster Linie auf meine Ansichten zu Community und Materialität bezogen.

Ich nahm an, dass meine Herangehensweise an das Thema Materialität im Bewerberpool einzigartig sein würde, einfach weil ich Erfahrungen mit einer Vielzahl von Verfahren hatte – von der traditionellen Möbelholzschnitzerei bis hin zur Roboterfertigung von Architekturkomponenten. Ein bisschen nachdenken musste ich über die Frage, wie meine Interaktion mit Design-Communities mich geprägt hat. Dabei kam ich zu einem neuen Verständnis für die Rolle von Community in meiner Praxis. In der Bewerbung schrieb ich über meine Erfahrungen mit Teamarbeit in unterschiedlichen Positionen – von der Leitung des Entwurfs einer Scheune für die Dilmun Hill Student Farm an der Cornell University bis hin zur Zusammenarbeit mit einer internationalen Gruppe von Studierenden, die in nur einer Woche einen Versammlungsraum auf einer abgelegenen Insel in Norwegen entwarfen und bauten. Ich beschrieb, wie diese Erfahrungen meine Herangehensweise an die Designarbeit verändert und mich darin bestärkt haben, in meinem Studio eine Kultur der Kooperation zu fördern, auch wenn ich mir dessen zu diesem Zeitpunkt noch nicht unmittelbar bewusst gewesen war.

Wie hast du dich gefühlt, als du erfahren hast, dass du angenommen wirst? Welche Erwartungen hattest du an das Fellowship?

Ich war schon ziemlich überrascht von der E-Mail, in der mir mitgeteilt wurde, dass ich angenommen bin. Die positive Antwort kam unerwartet, vor allem weil es schien, als sei die Welt zwischen meiner Bewerbung und der Antwort, in den ersten Monaten der COVID-Pandemie, zum Stillstand gekommen. Ich war hocherfreut zu erfahren, dass dieDAS nach wie vor bemüht war, ein Fellowship-Programm in jenem Jahr anzubieten. Folglich habe ich aufgeregt auf die äußerst seltene Gelegenheit gewartet, eine Reise über Ländergrenzen hinweg zu unternehmen, die mich in kreativer wie in pädagogischer Hinsicht weiterbringen würde.

Da es keine Geschichte des Programms gab, auf die ich hätte reagieren können, hatte ich zunächst auch keinerlei Erwartungen. Allerdings hoffte ich, dort auf sympathische und kenntnisreiche Personen zu treffen, die ganz andere Interessen und Erfahrungen als ich mitbringen würden.

Bitte nenne eine paar Höhepunkte aus deiner Zeit als Fellow.

Viele der geplanten Aktivitäten waren (in den meisten Fällen virtuelle) Begegnungen mit Designer*innen, Historiker*innen, Künstler*innen und Handwerker*innen aus der Region und darüber hinaus. Wir wollten mehr über ihre Arbeit erfahren und wie sie sich in ihrem Kontext positionierten. Das Meeting, das mir am stärksten in Erinnerung geblieben ist, war für mich ein Workshop mit einer Stuckateurin in Weimar, die auch natürliche Pigmente herstellte. Es war unglaublich inspirierend zu hören, woher sie ihre Pigmente bezieht, welche Beziehungen sie zu den Materialien und der Praxis hat und wie sie über Farben und Raum denkt.

Ein großer Teil der Zeit war für unsere eigene Designarbeit reserviert. Diese fand häufig in Zusammenarbeit mit anderen Fellows, aber auch mit dem Künstlerischen Leiter Maurizio Montalti statt. Am liebsten waren mir die Entwürfe zu einer Schaukel, die aus Holz, das uns ein örtliches Weingut gespendet hatte, entstehen sollte. Alle Fellows arbeiteten pflichtbewusst an der Aufarbeitung des Holzes, schreinerten die entsprechenden Verzahnungen und hängten die Schaukel dann vor Ort auf – und das alles in nur wenigen Tagen!

Noch ein weiterer Höhepunkt: Auch wenn die für uns geplanten Aktivitäten von Tag zu Tag variierten, so fanden wir doch während der Mahlzeiten in den Saalecker Werkstätten ausreichend Zeit für die Community. Alles war mit so viel Sorgfalt und Liebe selbst gekocht, dass sich dieser doch sehr fremde Ort für mich wie zu Hause anfühlte. Ich kann mich nicht daran erinnern, wie ich mich bei jedem einzelnen Treffen mit einer neuen Wissenschaftler*in oder Künstler*in gefühlt habe. Leider entsinne ich mich auch nicht aller Details der Exkursionen. Aber daran, wie ich den Frieden und das Familiäre an diesen Esstischen gespürt habe, erinnere ich mich sehr wohl, und wie es sich anfühlte, als ich mit den anderen Fellows und den dieDAS Mitarbeiter*innen um den Tisch saß, wie wir über unsere Pläne sprachen und die besten Augenblicke des Tages Revue passieren ließen.

Wie lebt die Erfahrung des Fellowships in dir weiter? Welche Auswirkungen haben sich bisher gezeigt?

Ich kam zur dieDAS bereits mit Produktionskenntnissen von mehreren Ausstellungen, und hatte viel Zeit auf Skulptur und Handwerk verwendet. Folglich hatte ich schon gewisse Erfahrungswerte in Bezug auf Materialien und Prozesse, die uns für die Arbeit zur Verfügung stehen. Als ich dann jedoch die übrigen Fellows kennengelernt und über ihre Arbeit etwas erfahren hatte, wurde mir bewusst, dass ich mich in meinem Handwerk bislang auf eine ziemlich begrenzte Anzahl von Materialpraktiken beschränkt hatte.

Mehr noch schockierte mich, dass ihre Praxis dort anfing, wo meine aufhörte. In ihren Ateliers arbeiteten einige der Fellows – ebenso wie der Künstlerische Leiter – mit Abfällen. Diese stammten entweder von anderen Designer*innen oder von Industrien, die keinen Gedanken an Abfallprodukte verschwenden, die sie in die Welt setzen. Von meinen Möbelprojekten her war ich es gewohnt, Reste aufzubewahren. Auch wusste ich, wie man Ton recycelt. Dass man aber den Staub einer Schleifmaschine verwenden kann, um damit Myzelkulturen zu füttern, oder das man Marmorpulver von Skulpturen sammelt und dieses in den Ton für handgefertigte Figuren einbringen kann, das waren für mich neue und aufregende Entdeckungen. Und die habe ich weiterverfolgt, als ich wieder nach Hause zurückgekehrt bin.

Ich denke jedes Mal an das Fellowship an der dieDAS, wenn ich meine Werkstatt saubermache, jedes Mal, wenn ich ein Stückchen Stein von einer Skulptur abschlage. Denn meine Erfahrung dort hat mich dazu angeregt, kreatives Potenzial noch im kleinsten Stück Material zu sehen, einschließlich dem Staub an meinen Füßen.

Wie konntest du deine Erfahrung als Fellow dann in der Arbeit für die Jury nutzen?

Es war mir eine Ehre, 2023 als Jury-Mitglied eingeladen zu werden. Mit großem Enthusiasmus machte ich mich daran, die Vielzahl von Bewerbungen zu evaluieren. Durch meine Erfahrung als dieDAS Fellow wusste ich, dass ich nach Bewerber*innen Ausschau halten musste, deren Arbeit schon über einen längeren Zeitraum wirklich genau zum Thema des Fellowships passte. Jeder kann eine Bewerbung so schreiben, dass sie zu einem Thema passt, aber wahres Engagement für einen Prozess oder eine Arbeitsweise lässt sich nur durch jahrelang anhaltendes Interesse, permanente Weiterbildung und kontinuierliches Experimentieren dokumentieren.

Ich wusste auch, dass es wichtig war, ein Spektrum von Fellows auszuwählen, deren Schwerpunkte hinreichend abwechslungsreich sind, sodass sie voneinander lernen und einander herausfordern können. Das ist nötig, weil es der Künstlerischen Leitung wichtig ist, aus der Vielfalt Impulse für die gemeinsame Arbeit vor Ort zu ziehen. Vor allem ist es jedoch entscheidend, dass die Fellows voneinander lernen. Man täte der Lernerfahrung keinen Gefallen, wenn alle sich über sämtliche Aspekte ihrer Arbeitsweisen einig wären.

Zu guter Letzt war ich während meiner Zeit als Fellow in Saaleck im Jahr 2020 der mit deutlichem Abstand jüngste Fellow. Daher empfand ich es als wichtig, für jene jungen Designer*innen zu sprechen, die vielleicht noch nicht so viel in ihren Mappen und Lebensläufen vorzuweisen, die aber doch Leidenschaft und vielversprechendes Talent in ihrer bisherigen Arbeit gezeigt hatten. Die Vision der dieDAS widmet sich der Zukunft des Designs, und darum glaube ich, dass Fellows jeden Alters nötig sind, um ihre Generationen in eine nachhaltigere, kooperative und ethische Zukunft zu führen.

Wie war deine Zusammenarbeit mit den anderen Jurymitgliedern?

Die Diskussionen waren effizient, durchdacht und kollegial. Nach meiner Erfahrung als Fellow hatte ich von der dieDAS nichts anderes erwartet. Dennoch war ich froh festzustellen, dass meine Stimme so viel Gewicht hatte wie die jedes anderen Mitglieds in der Jury. Auch respektierten die anderen Mitglieder meine Erfahrung als Fellow und was ich davon abgeleitet zu unserer Diskussion beitragen konnte.

Wir sichteten zunächst sämtliche Bewerbungen unabhängig voneinander. Dann wurden Punkte verteilt gemäß einer Matrix, die das dieDAS Team zuvor verteilt hatte. Diese Punkte wurden schließlich addiert und ein Durchschnitt ermittelt. Auf dieser Grundlage sind wir dann in die Diskussion mit den Bewerbungen mit der höchsten Punktzahl eingestiegen und gingen über mehrere Stunden die Liste nach und nach durch.

Ich kann mich daran erinnern, dass unsere Jury sehr rasch zu einem breiten Konsens für zwei Kandidat*innen aufgrund ihrer hohen Punktzahl kam. Die Punkte der nachfolgenden Kandidat*innen waren jedoch mehr oder weniger gleich. Daher verbrachten wir viel Zeit damit, den Argumenten zuzuhören, mit denen sich alle für die Bewerber*innen aussprachen, die ihnen jeweils am interessantesten erschienen. Letztlich waren wir uns wohl bewusst, dass alle Kandidat*innen, über die wir diskutierten, sich gut als Fellows eignen würden. Die endgültige Entscheidung haben wir dann dem Künstlerischen Leiter überlassen, der mit den Finalist*innen noch persönliche Interviews geführt hat.

Wie erhoffst du dir die zukünftige Entwicklung des Programms?

Ich freue mich auf den Tag, an dem ich die Saalecker Werkstätten besuchen und eine große, lebhafte Gemeinschaft von Designerinnen und Designern erleben kann, die sich leidenschaftlich mit Experimenten zu Material, Technik und Prozess beschäftigt. Ich hoffe, dass die Erweiterung des Fellowship-Programms das Gefühl familiärer Nähe bewahren kann, die ich gemeinsam mit den anderen drei Fellows des Auftaktjahres erlebt habe.

Die Ziele des Programms sind ehrgeizig, und ich bin davon überzeugt, dass die folgenden Generationen von Fellows die architektonische Erweiterung sowie die Renovierung der vorhandenen Gebäude sehr zu schätzen wissen werden. Unsere kleine Gruppe der ersten Fellows hat jedoch eine besonders enge Bindung ermöglicht, als wir in den alten Gemäuern übernachteten, uns um einen kleinen Esstisch drängten und gemeinsam die Anfangsphasen des Programms mitgestalteten. Ich hoffe, dass diese besondere Verbindung auch bei den zukünftigen Teilnehmer*innen des dieDAS Fellowship-Programms nicht verloren gehen.

Ich glaube, das Ziel der dieDAS besteht gerade darin, eine neue Design-Community zu schaffen – und zwar eine, die auf Vertrauen und Kooperation zwischen den Fellows und ihrer Umgebung basiert. Diese Community strebt danach, die Gesellschaft durch Innovationen in den Bereichen Design, Architektur, Handwerk und Kunst zu verbessern. Zudem ist sie eine Gemeinschaft, in der kreative und produktive Beziehungen weit über die Dauer der Fellowships hinaus Bestand haben.

Ich weiß, dass das dieDAS Team hart daran arbeiten wird, diese Ziele umzusetzen. Vieles hängt dabei jedoch auch vom Charakter der Fellows ab sowie von den Erfahrungen, die sie vor Ort machen. Es ist meine Hoffnung, dass zukünftige Partner*innen des Programms im Laufe der Jahre ein Programm kuratieren, das dieses Gefühl der Kollegialität unter den Fellows fördert und bewahrt.

EPILOG UND DANK

Mit *Monumental Affairs_Living with Contested Spaces* liegt die erste Publikation der Design Akademie Saaleck vor. Dieser Auftaktband der neuen Reihe *dieDASdocs* präsentiert die Ergebnisse des dieDAS Fellowships 2023 und des anschließenden dieDAS walk + talk Symposiums unter der Künstlerischen Leitung des renommierten US-amerikanischen Architekten Germane Barnes, dessen Charisma, Gelassenheit und intellektuelle Kraft mich stark beeindruckt haben. Ihm gilt mein ganz besonderer Dank für seinen Mut und seine Neugierde im Umgang mit dem „unbequemen Denkmal" in Saaleck. Mit *Monumental Affairs* untersucht Germane die Komplexität von Denkmalen auch im internationalen Kontext und verhandelt drängende Themen wie Rasse, Ethnizität, Nationalismus, Architektur und Demokratie an einem historisch kontaminierten Schauplatz. Er hat sich sowohl mit den Mechanismen der Konstruktion von Denkmalen und dem Prozess ihrer Kanonisierung auseinandergesetzt als auch in Kooperation mit den teilnehmenden Designer*innen, Architekt*innen, Kritiker*innen und Aktivist*innen den inhaltlichen Rahmen für ein produktives Programm geschaffen. Ihnen allen und ihrem engagierten Austausch ist der vorliegende Band zu verdanken.

Als ich am 3. Dezember 2015 das allererste Mal vor den verschlossenen Toren der Saalecker Werkstätten stand, hat mich der Blick durch die Gitterstäbe auf das über der Saale thronende Haupthaus mit Schrecken erfüllt und zeitgleich fasziniert. Das unsanierte, leerstehende Gebäudeensemble wirkte fast verträumt und verwunschen, und doch wusste ich, dass sich hier an diesem entlegenen Ort im südlichen Sachsen-Anhalt während der dunkelsten Epoche der deutschen Geschichte politische und gesellschaftliche Größen die Klinke in die Hand gegeben hatten – Hitler, Goebbels, Frick, Darré und viele mehr. Sie alle waren der Einladung des damaligen Hausherrn Paul Schultze-Naumburg gefolgt, um in Saaleck ihre finsteren Ideen auszutauschen und Pläne des Bösen zu schmieden.

Seit dieser ersten Begegnung lässt mich Saaleck nicht mehr los. Als ich zwei Jahre später über meinen Studienfreund Stephan Kujas erfuhr, dass die ehemaligen Saalecker Werkstätten zum Verkauf stehen, ergriff ich die Gelegenheit und vereinbarte zunächst aus reiner Neugierde einen Besichtigungstermin. Während meines Masterstudiums „Schutz Europäischer Kulturgüter" an der Europa-Universität Viadrina in Frankfurt

(Oder) unter Prof. Paul Zalewski hatte ich mich intensiv mit „unbequemen Denkmalen" beschäftigt, zum Obersalzberg geforscht und geschrieben sowie als Projektarbeit einen Film über den Umgang mit dem Bückeberg bei Hameln gedreht, dem Schauplatz der sogenannten Reichserntedankfeste. Diese propagandistisch inszenierten Events waren die größten Massenveranstaltungen des „Dritten Reichs" nach den Reichsparteitagen in Nürnberg, mit dem Unterschied, dass die Spuren der Vergangenheit am Bückeberg nur noch wenig erkennbar sind und es bis dato keine gewissenhafte Auseinandersetzung mit dem Ort und seiner Geschichte gegeben hat. Einige Bereiche des einst riesigen Areals waren inzwischen mit Einfamilienhäusern bebaut worden, in einem Versuch, die schwerwiegende Vergangenheit des Ortes zu überformen.

Ähnliches hatte der Vorbesitzer der Saalecker Werkstätten im Sinn, als er die Anlage Mitte der 1990er-Jahre erwarb. Mit der Umwandlung in einen Hotelkomplex sollten kommerzielle Interessen in den Vordergrund gerückt werden, ohne sich mit der kontaminierten Geschichte auseinanderzusetzen oder sie gar bewusst zu thematisieren. Und auch die Verkaufsbroschüre von 2017 betonte, dass sich „mit dieser Immobilie eine sehr interessante Kombination aus landwirtschaftlicher und architektonischer Schönheit sowie betriebswirtschaftlichem Nutzen" böte, zeichne sich das „unvergleichliche Anwesen" doch aus durch „eine ganzheitliche Ästhetik, die schöpferisches Weiterdenken aus kulturlandschaftlichem Erbe anstrebte". „Insbesondere die ‚natürliche' Terrasse direkt oberhalb der Saale mit herrlichem Blick über den Fluss und die umliegende Kulturlandschaft laden zur Gestaltung besonderer Plätze ein." Kein Wort darüber, dass diesen Blick auch Adolf Hitler mit Wonne genoss, der auf Einladung des Bauherrn Paul Schultze-Naumburg die Saalecker Werkstätten schon Anfang der 1930er-Jahre besuchte.

Während dieser ersten Besichtigung der Anlage am 15. Mai 2017 und der Erkundung der Haupt- und Nebengebäude mit ihrer zum Teil obskuren Architektur sowie den zahlreichen verwinkelten Treppenhäusern und Fluren, Kammern und Sälen hat mich neben den imposanten Gesellschaftsräumen besonders die Küche in ihren Bann gezogen. In dieser Küche wurden auch die Speisen für die Elite des Nationalsozialismus zubereitet, ebenso wie für die Bewohner und Bewohnerinnen des Altenheims, das später und bis 1995 in den Saalecker Werkstätten untergebracht war und bis heute das kollektive Gedächtnis des Dorfes prägt.

Als ich die Küche im Untergeschoss des Anbaus von 1925 menschenleer und verlassen durchquerte, kam mir die Idee, dass das Herzstück der Saalecker Werkstätten in Zukunft wieder eine Rolle spielen könnte, und dies in einem vollkommen neuen, inklusiven und demokratischen Rahmen. Und mit dieser noch vagen Grundidee habe ich kurze Zeit später bei Egidio Marzona angeklopft.

Egidio Marzona ist ein Freund, den ich zutiefst bewundere. Er hat über Jahrzehnte eine der wichtigsten Kunstsammlungen des Landes geschaffen, einen einzigartigen Skulpturengarten in den italienischen Bergen ermöglicht und mit dem Archiv der Avantgarden (AdA) in Dresden der Welt ein einzigartiges Archiv geschenkt. Fast zwei Millionen Archivalien werden hier sukzessive erfasst und digitalisiert. Jedes einzelne Stück ist durch Egidios Hände gegangen, er kann zu jedem Blatt Papier, jedem Brief, jedem Buch, Bild, Stuhl oder Plakat einen Vortrag halten und das Objekt kunst- und kulturhistorisch einordnen. Das Wissen dieses Mannes ist phänomenal, ebenso sein Vorstellungsvermögen. Und so erkannte er sofort die Möglichkeiten, die sich durch eine Transformation der Saalecker Werkstätten ergeben könnten und machte mit. Ohne seine Weitsicht, sein Wissen und seine Ressourcen würde es das Projekt in Saaleck nicht geben. Egidio gilt mein innigster Dank, meine größte Bewunderung.

2018 gründeten wir gemeinsam mit dem Rechtsanwalt Andreas Silbersack, unserem dritten Vorstandsmitglied, die Marzona Stiftung Neue Saalecker Werkstätten. Auch Andreas ist ein Visionär, dem die Entwicklung seines Bundeslandes Sachsen-Anhalt am Herzen liegt. Der gebürtige Hallenser ist gesellschaftlich und politisch außergewöhnlich vielseitig engagiert und sieht, wie schon Egidio, die Chancen eines zivilgesellschaftlichen Engagements in Saaleck am südlichsten Zipfel des Landes – in einer Region, die sich nicht nur durch ihre landschaftliche Schönheit, sondern vor allem auch durch ihre extrem hohe Dichte an ultrarechten Wählern und Wählerinnen auszeichnet. Genau hier wollen wir ein Zeichen setzen, Demokratie stärken, Dialog fördern, in Gemeinschaft Neues gestalten.

Mit diesem Ziel vor Augen und der tatkräftigen Unterstützung des damaligen Bundestagsabgeordneten Rüdiger Kruse bekamen wir die entscheidenden Zusagen sowohl für Fördermittel des Bundes als auch für eine Anschubfinanzierung des Landes Sachsen-Anhalt. Auch Ministerpräsident Reiner Haseloff, Staatsminister für Kultur und Chef der Staatskanzlei Sachsen-Anhalt, Rainer Robra, und der heutige Landtagspräsident Dr. Gunnar Schellenberger unterstützten die einzigartige Public Private Partnership mit der Marzona Stiftung und ermöglichten 2019 die Gründung der dieDAS. Deren Name geht auf eine Eingebung des Journalisten Niklas Maak zurück, der nach einer gemeinsamen Besichtigung der Saalecker Werkstätten vorschlug, das neue Projekt einfach Design Akademie Saaleck zu nennen – kurz dieDAS.

Und jetzt kommt Tatjana Sprick ins Spiel, die schon seit der allerersten Gründungsphase 2018 den inhaltlichen und strukturellen Aufbau der Akademie maßgeblich mit begleitet. Durch ihre Kenntnis der internationalen Designwelt, ihr breites Netzwerk und ihre Leidenschaft für Menschen und Design hat sie dieDAS entscheidend geprägt. Als Direktorin für Programm und Entwicklung ist es Tatjana zu verdanken, dass Maurizio Montalti 2020 als erster künstlerischer Leiter über drei Jahre das dieDAS Fellowship-Programm mit konzipiert und mit entwickelt hat, bevor sie Germane Barnes für diese Position begeistern konnte, ebenso wie einige der interessantesten internationalen Designer*innen und Architekt*innen, die dieDAS in Saaleck als Mentor*innen, Speaker und Mitwirkende unterstützen.

Die außergewöhnliche gegenwartkulturelle Transformation der Saalecker Werkstätten ist das Ergebnis einer klaren Vision, harter Arbeit, Hartnäckigkeit und Durchhaltevermögen. Vor allem aber ist es das Werk vieler, die ein gemeinsames Ziel vor Augen haben – das Reframing des „unbequemen Denkmals" in einen Ort der Innovation und des Austauschs, divers, interdisziplinär, demokratisch und offen. Ich danke der dänischen Architektin Dorte Mandrup, deren Masterplan für die Restaurierung in Saaleck der dieDAS einen für die Zukunft angemessenen Rahmen schafft, ebenso wie unseren Kuratoriumsmitgliedern Omer Arbel, Christian Benimana, Prof. Bettina Erzgräber, Hella Jongerius, Maurizio Montalti und Prof. M. Whiting für ihr Engagement, ihren Rat und ihre guten Ideen. Dank geht auch an Johanna Söhningen und Dr. Rainer Schmitz, die durch ihre Forschung unser Projekt wissenschaftlich begleiten, an unsere Mitarbeiterinnen Caroline Rebel und Olga Durandina sowie an Andra Schumann für ihre fachkundige Unterstützung bei der Umsetzung des Bauvorhabens. Ein herzlicher Dank geht auch an die Autor*innen des vorliegenden Bandes, an unsere äußerst präzisen und aufmerksamen Redakteurinnen und Designexpertinnen Anna Carnick und Wava Carpenter, wie auch an die talentierten Gestalterinnen Francesca Biagiotti und Francesca Pellicciari vom Studio Pupilla, an Lena Kiessler vom Hatje Cantz Verlag für die großartige Idee, mit *dieDASdocs* eine fortlaufende Reihe zu schaffen. Dank geht auch an Dorothee Hahn für die geschickte Koordination des Projekts. Ich danke den Patrons der Marzona Stiftung Neue Saalecker Werkstätten, dass sie an dieses Projekt glauben und den Mitarbeitern der Staatskanzlei in Magdeburg, Ingo Mundt, Tom Altenburg und René Richter, für ihren besonderen Einsatz, ebenso wie Dr. Joachim Scherrieble und Harald Behne vom Landesverwaltungsamt für die lösungsorientierte und pragmatische Begleitung. Ich richte meinen Dank auch an die Fördermittelgeber von Land und Bund, der Bundeskulturstiftung, die diesen Band ermöglicht hat, und an unseren wachsenden Kreis von Sponsoren und Partnern. Der Oberbürgermeister der Stadt Naumburg, Armin Müller, ist für dieDAS und die Marzona Stiftung ein vertrauter Wegbegleiter und Förderer geworden, der mit seiner Einladung zum „mayor's lunch" alljährlich unsere walk+talk Gäste auf ihrem Rundgang durch Naumburg verwöhnt.

Gerade liegen die Bewerbungsunterlagen für das 6. Fellowship-Programm im Sommer 2024 auf meinem Schreibtisch. Germane Barnes wird mit seinem neuen Thema *Material Evidence – The Absence of Land and Labor* wieder eine hochmotivierte Gruppe innovativer und mutiger Designer*innen, Architekt*innen und Handwerker*innen in Saaleck versammeln. An allererster Stelle ist es diesen jungen Talenten zu verdanken, dass dieDAS sich zu dem Ort entwickelt, den wir uns vorgestellt haben, zu dem Ort, an dem wir auf das Fundament einer schwer wiegenden Vergangenheit etwas Konstruktives und Kollektives aufbauen und nach besseren, innovativen Lösungsansätzen für unsere gemeinsame Zukunft suchen. Danke an alle dieDAS Fellows für die Verwirklichung dieser Vision. Und danke an Andrea Sprick und Oscar Casas Pinto, dass sie uns während der Fellowships in Saaleck so liebevoll umsorgen, an unseren Facility Manager Ralf König und unseren Nachbarn Karl-Heinz Tischner, ohne den die Linden im Garten nicht zu bändigen wären. Die Baugenehmigung für die Sanierung der Anlage liegt vor, die Fördermittel stehen bereit. 2024 geht das Projekt in die nächste Phase, und ich bin zutiefst demütig und dankbar, dass ich dabei sein darf.

Arne Cornelius Wasmuth

Editor
Marzona Stiftung Neue Saalecker Werkstätten

Managing editors
Anna Carnick, Wava Carpenter

Project management
Dorothee Hahn

Copyediting
Irene Schaudies (English), Ilka Backmeister-Collacott (German)

Translations from the German
Amy Klement

Translations from the English
Volker Ellerbeck

Graphic design
Studio Pupilla

Production
Alise Ausmane, Hatje Cantz

Reproductions
DLG Graphic, Paris

Printing and binding
DZS Grafik d.o.o., Ljubljana

Funded by

Supporters
We would like to thank our generous supporters, who contributed unstintingly to making this forward-looking project a success:

Artek
Auto Center Chemnitz
Bocci
Dr. Hauschka
Emily Asset Management
Freifrau Manufaktur
Hotel Goldener Löwe Betriebsgesellschaft
Lintex
Nietzsche-Haus
Peppermint Holding
Stadt Naumburg
Winzervereinigung Freyburg-Unstrut

Published by
Hatje Cantz Verlag GmbH
Mommsenstraße 27
10629 Berlin
Germany
www.hatjecantz.de
A Ganske Publishing Group Company

ISBN (print) 978-3-7757-5655-6
ISBN (PDF) 978-3-7757-5743-0

Printed in Slovenia

Image credits

1–15 Photos © dieDAS – Design Akademie Saaleck **16** Photo: Lyndon French; courtesy of Studio Barnes **17** Photo: Claudia Rossini; courtesy of Studio Barnes **18** Photo © dieDAS – Design Akademie Saaleck **19** Image courtesy of Bryan C. Lee, Jr. **20** Image courtesy of Bryan C. Lee, Jr., and Colloqate Design **21** Photo: Edmund Sumner; courtesy of New South **22** Photo courtesy of New South **23** Photo © dieDAS – Design Akademie Saaleck **24** Source unknown **25–28** Photos © dieDAS – Design Akademie Saaleck **29–34** Images by and courtesy of Dorte Mandrup **35** Source unknown **36** First published in Deutsche Bauzeitung 46 (1929), p. 401 **37** and **38** Photos © dieDAS – Design Akademie Saaleck **39** Photo: Guido Siebert; courtesy of dieDAS – Design Akademie Saaleck **40–42** Photos © dieDAS – Design Akademie Saaleck **43–45** Images by and courtesy of Dorte Mandrup **46–49** Photos © dieDAS – Design Akademie Saaleck **50** Photo © Maurizio Montalti **51–62** Photos © dieDAS – Design Akademie Saaleck **63** Photo: James Harris; courtesy of Design Miami **64** Photo © dieDAS – Design Akademie Saaleck **65** Photo © dieDAS – Design Akademie Saaleck **66** Photo © Maurizio Montalti **67** Photo © dieDAS – Design Akademie Saaleck **68** Photo © Maurizio Montalti **69–77** Photos © dieDAS – Design Akademie Saaleck **78** Photo © Arne Cornelius Wasmuth **79** Photo © Tatjana Sprick **80–83** Photos © dieDAS – Design Akademie Saaleck